ALNWICK CASTLE

THE HOME OF THE DUKE AND DUCHESS OF NORTHUMBERLAND

ALNWICK CASTLE

THE HOME OF THE DUKE AND DUCHESS OF NORTHUMBERLAND

James McDonald

F

FRANCES LINCOLN LIMITED
PUBLISHERS

To my nephew and nieces,
Thomas, Sophie and Lucy McDonald

'I would like to dedicate this book
to Patrick Garner (1954–2010), with
gratitude and fond memories.'
The Duchess of Northumberland

Frances Lincoln Limited
4 Torriano Mews
Torriano Avenue
London NW5 2RZ
www.franceslincoln.com

Alnwick Castle
Copyright © Frances Lincoln Limited 2012
Text copyright © James McDonald 2012
Photographs copyright © James McDonald 2012 with the exception of
those listed on page 240
First Frances Lincoln edition 2012

A catalogue record for this book is available from the British Library.

ISBN 9-780-7112-3237-2

Printed and bound in China

9 8 7 6 5 4 3 2

ENDPAPERS Detail of Montiroli's cinquecento-style ceiling in the Drawing Room.
PAGE 1 In the Italian style, Giovanni Tacca Iozzi carved the Roman god of wine, Bacchus
   on the chimneypiece of the Drawing Room.
PAGES 2–3 Looking westwards from the Duchess's Seat, along the 'Capability' Brown
   landscape around the River Aln and at the Lion Bridge by James Adam. Hulne Park
   and Alnwick Moor are in the far distance.
RIGHT The 4th Duke's cinquecento-style Drawing Room displays extremely rare
   survivors from Louis XIV's Palace of Versailles, the 1683 Baroque Cucci cabinets.
FAR RIGHT A Chinese *famille-rose* basin from the Qainlong period in the Drawing Room.

CONTENTS

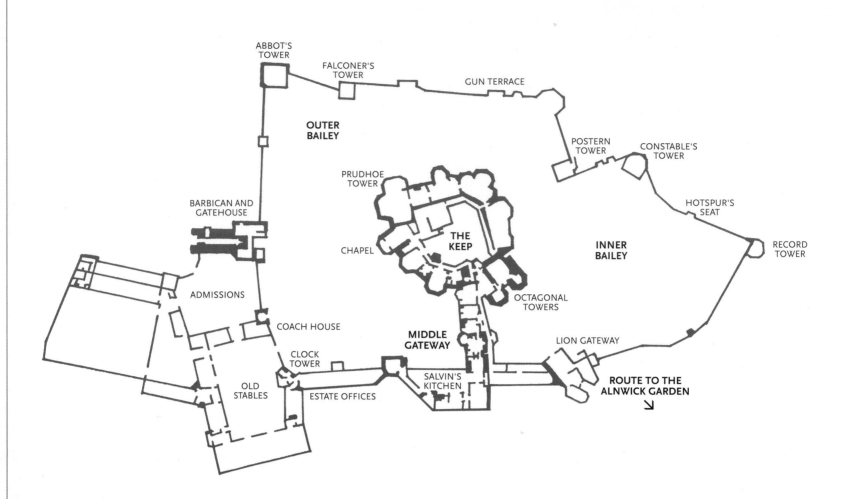

ABBOT'S
TOWER

FALCONER'S
TOWER

GUN TERRACE

OUTER
BAILEY

POSTERN
TOWER

CONSTABLE'S
TOWER

BARBICAN AND
GATEHOUSE

PRUDHOE
TOWER

HOTSPUR'S
SEAT

THE KEEP

INNER
BAILEY

RECORD
TOWER

CHAPEL

ADMISSIONS

OCTAGONAL
TOWERS

COACH HOUSE

MIDDLE
GATEWAY

LION GATEWAY

CLOCK
TOWER

OLD
STABLES

SALVIN'S
KITCHEN

ROUTE TO THE
ALNWICK GARDEN

ESTATE OFFICES

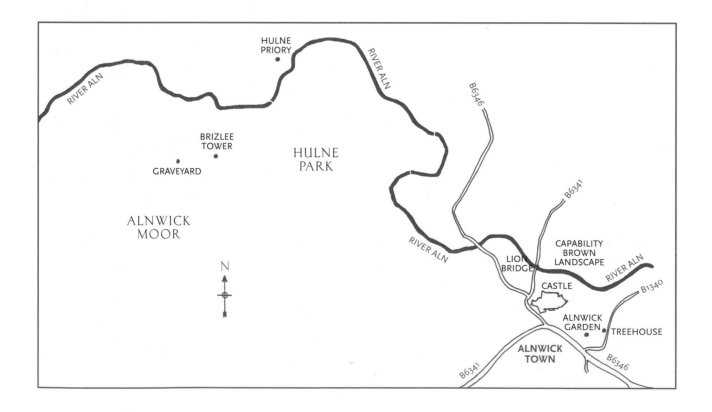

RIVER ALN

HULNE
PRIORY

RIVER ALN

B6346

RIVER ALN

BRIZLEE
TOWER

HULNE
PARK

GRAVEYARD

B6341

ALNWICK
MOOR

CAPABILITY
BROWN
LANDSCAPE

N

RIVER ALN

RIVER ALN

LION
BRIDGE

CASTLE

B1340

ALNWICK
GARDEN

TREEHOUSE

ALNWICK
TOWN

B6341

B6346

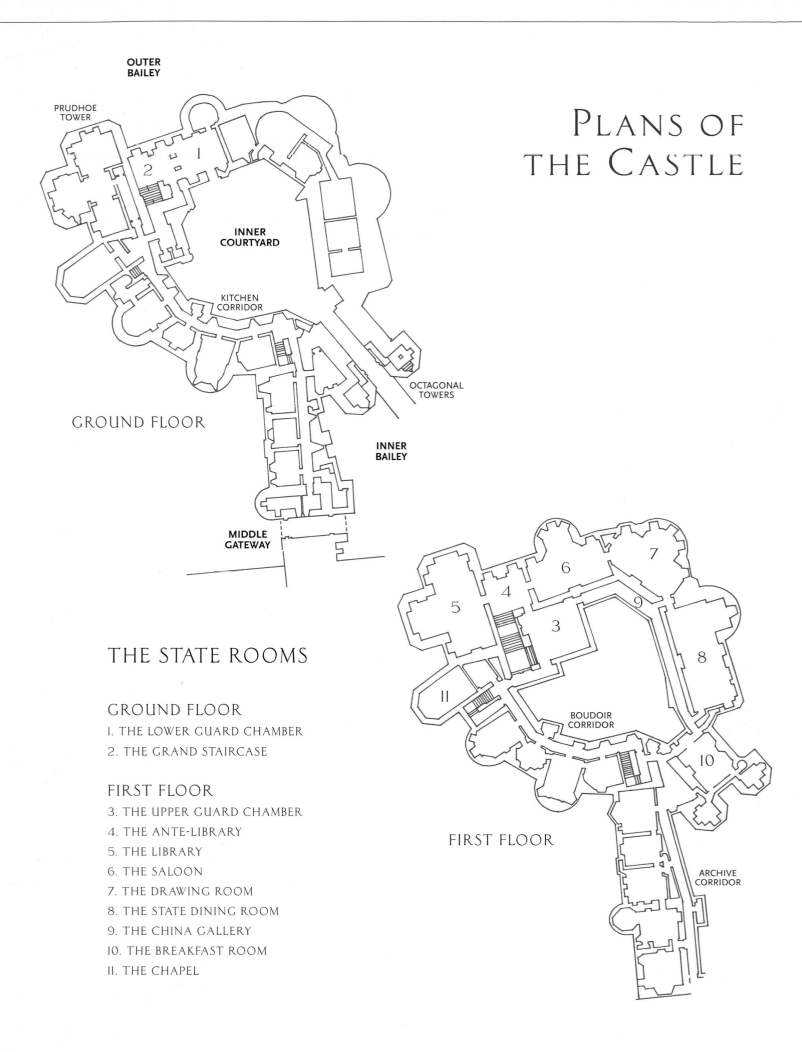

PLANS OF THE CASTLE

OUTER BAILEY

PRUDHOE TOWER

INNER COURTYARD

KITCHEN CORRIDOR

GROUND FLOOR

OCTAGONAL TOWERS

INNER BAILEY

MIDDLE GATEWAY

6
7
4
5
9
3
11
8
BOUDOIR CORRIDOR
10

FIRST FLOOR

ARCHIVE CORRIDOR

THE STATE ROOMS

GROUND FLOOR
1. THE LOWER GUARD CHAMBER
2. THE GRAND STAIRCASE

FIRST FLOOR
3. THE UPPER GUARD CHAMBER
4. THE ANTE-LIBRARY
5. THE LIBRARY
6. THE SALOON
7. THE DRAWING ROOM
8. THE STATE DINING ROOM
9. THE CHINA GALLERY
10. THE BREAKFAST ROOM
11. THE CHAPEL

FOREWORD

BY THE DUCHESS OF NORTHUMBERLAND

ALNWICK CASTLE has been a wonderful home to generations of Dukes of Northumberland and their Percy children. Each generation has used it differently and loved it for its amazing art and furniture collection, its sense of history and its staggering views. My husband Ralph and I readily acknowledge that the castle will always be more important than its occupants, and rightly so. Dukes and their families will come and go, leaving a small imprint on their home, but the walls of the castle remain solid and unchanged.

When we moved to Alnwick in 1995 we knew the task which lay before us. Most importantly, we wanted to create a home for our four children. We wanted to update the castle, prevent it from becoming a museum and make it so perfect and so comfortable that future generations would never want to live anywhere else. First we created a huge kitchen which would become the 'heart' of the castle. Everyone looking for us knows they'll probably find us in the kitchen – as in most homes in the twenty-first century. From the kitchen, we made our plans to upgrade, re-roof and restore Alnwick Castle.

I once said, jokingly, to the Clerk of Works that I would associate our time at Alnwick with one word: scaffolding. He looked horrified but I meant it as a compliment. Scaffolding shows that improvements are ongoing and that someone is caring for the fabric of the building. Ralph and I are determined to pass Alnwick Castle on to the next generation in the best possible condition so that they can enjoy it, encourage future generations to love it and make their own improvements without having to worry about a leaking roof. We have almost finished the task we set ourselves and we are now moving towards a similar restoration of Syon House in London.

I think I was fortunate to have a husband who allowed me a completely free rein to do what I wanted to do so long as it remained 'in budget'. We subconsciously established clear boundaries from our early days at Alnwick. He didn't get involved indoors and I didn't interfere with what he was doing out of doors. The improvements he has made to the landscape and Hulne Park are staggering and I believe our unofficial arrangement has worked in Alnwick's favour. The financial climate was also hugely beneficial: we could never have embarked on such a programme in a period of recession.

At the same time as we were beginning the castle restoration I had begun to work with a design team, engineers, builders, quantity surveyors, cost consultants and project managers to build the Alnwick Garden, a huge, public charitable project that was to benefit the local community. I learned so much from my daily involvement with the garden project, which was to prove useful with the ongoing work in the castle. I learned to delegate and I also learned to seek out the best advice, to listen carefully to that advice and then to have the strength of conviction to make my own decisions. I learned not to worry what people thought of me – an important attribute when making changes of any kind.

We had a fantastic team of craftsmen to support us, who opened my eyes to what was possible. We had some hairy moments along the way and some funny moments too. Patrick Garner, the household controller to whom this book is dedicated, helped me every step of the way. The quality of the work undertaken at Alnwick Castle is a testament to the expertise and knowledge of those staff at Northumberland Estates who never settled for second best. I had the easy job: I simply relied upon being pointed in the right direction by a team of people who knew more than I did. Ralph has always loved Alnwick, which was his childhood home, but I have to admit that I saw Alnwick primarily as a job that needed to be done. That job has been all but completed: our eldest son loves the castle and I am confident that, in the future, it will continue to flourish in his hands.

I would like to thank James McDonald, who has written and taken most of the excellent photographs for this record of Alnwick Castle (occasionally driving us mad in the process!).

RIGHT The Duchess with her eldest son, George, Earl Percy.
(Copyright © Mark Mather 2011)

INTRODUCTION

THE DUKE AND DUCHESS OF NORTHUMBERLAND head one of the United Kingdom's wealthiest and most aristocratic dynasties. As members of the Percy family they trace their roots back to 1066 and beyond.

Unlike some other dukedoms, their name, Northumberland, is also that of the county in which the Duke and Duchess live at Alnwick – pronounced 'Annick', rhyming with panic. On the Scottish border in the north-east of England, the castle sits on a hill above the River Aln, which after 5 miles/8 kilometres flows past Alnmouth into the North Sea. Standing on the north-east edge of the town of Alnwick, it is reminiscent of Windsor Castle, though smaller. You drive in through a forbidding military gatehouse, into the lawned Outer Bailey; then you pass the Inner Bailey, with more lawns, under the Octagonal Towers into an enclosed courtyard and the Keep. On the front door of the castle hangs the biggest knocker you have ever seen.

The castle's external layout is more or less the same as it was in the twelfth century. While many English stately homes are only a few hundred years old, perhaps sitting on the ruins of a more defensive manor house linking them to the medieval era, this is not the case with Alnwick Castle; it remains a massive medieval feudal fortress. The castle's purpose was a strategic one: to defend the northern border of the kingdom of England from the Scots; or, as the Scots saw it, as a base from which the English could threaten and be aggressive towards them. Domestic comfort was of secondary importance.

On a photographic shoot at the castle in 2009 for *World of Interiors* magazine, I was with the 'all-seeing' Jessica Haynes, and she wondered where all the feudal furniture had gone. At the time, I had no idea either. The short answer is that the family fought bloody battles for hundreds of years against the Scots, and sometimes against monarchs. They lived between many homes – including, at various times, the castles of Alnwick, Warkworth and Prudhoe in Northumberland, those of Spofforth and Wressil in Yorkshire, and Petworth House in Sussex – and carted their chattels from place to place. By the eighteenth century, the castle was more or less uninhabitable, the male line had ceased and the feudal furniture was scattered.

What we see inside the castle today is the result of three major restorations over the last few hundred years and distilled from the sale of houses owned by the family over the last 150 years. The Percys were not just rich: they were very rich. While houses had to be disposed of, many of the contents of Warkworth and Kielder Castles in Northumberland, Albury House in Surrey, Stanwick Park in Yorkshire and Northumberland House in London are now at Alnwick Castle. It is a full house.

Some Percys showed enthusiasm for collecting, in particular the 9th Earl, who amassed books; Algernon, the 10th Earl, who liked Old Masters as well as Van Dyck and Lely; and Charles, the 6th Duke of Somerset, and his Percy wife Duchess Elizabeth, who loved the painter William Dobson. The 1st Duchess of Northumberland hoovered up Flemish bargains on her Continental travels and her husband's acquisitions reflect his liking for Canaletto, the sculptor Wilton and the cabinet-makers Chippendale and Linnell. The 3rd Duke was a patron of the furniture-makers Morel and Hughes and fancied silver gilt, while his brother, the 4th Duke, bought the Camuccini Collection, which included works by Bellini, Raphael, Guido Reni, Andrea del Sarto, Badalocchio and Claude – probably one of the greatest single art purchases ever made by an Englishman abroad.

In the eighteenth century the 1st Duchess, Elizabeth, restored the castle, turning it into a proper country residence. In the mid-nineteenth century the extensive work of Algernon, the 4th Duke, resulted in the semi-Roman cinquecento-style Victorian state rooms we see today. The current Duchess's restoration of the interior honours the work of these two great Percys: she could not have been more sensitive to the fabric and history of the castle her husband inherited. It is now a fine example of 'British country house meeting sixteenth-century Roman palace', as I hope this book will show. Before taking you on a tour of the castle, however, to understand what we see today and where this family got its power and ducal titles from, it is necessary to outline the history of the Percy ancestors.

Money matters here. For those who own land and what is under it, the agricultural revolution in the eighteenth century,

the industrial revolution in the nineteenth century, two world wars in the twentieth century and the prosperity of the post-1980s Thatcher years were directly aligned to their fortunes, and this family is no exception. Fluctuating fortunes mean that the story includes one Duke and Duchess in the 1850s gutting the castle and spending in today's terms millions of pounds and, a hundred years later, another Duchess fighting her husband to replace a worn carpet.

Obviously I could not interview Harry Hotspur, the Percy who appears in Shakespeare's plays, or the Percy who tried to blow up the Houses of Parliament during the Gunpowder Plot. However, the 1st Duchess kept one of the most fascinating journals of the eighteenth century and I have been able to draw on that. I had tea with the wife of the 10th Duke, now the Dowager Duchess and aged eighty-nine when I interviewed her, and have recounted some of her anecdotes. I have also relied heavily on my conversations with the Duke and Duchess, in the hope of leaving their imprint on this book.

We shall see that the current Duke's blood descends from a 1066 Percy, mostly via the male line but twice via Percy women. The Percy story includes an excessive number of heirs, with

seventeen called Henry. Their valiant history is intertwined with the drama of English history, from early times to later nationhood, and especially of the monarchy. The tale is of almost a thousand years of Britain seen through the aristocratic prism of one family for whom Alnwick Castle is, and continues to be, home.

A constant theme in all my interviews with the Duchess is her love for her family, over whom she stands guard with lioness-like ferocity. To her the ultimate achievement, the desire that both she and the Duke talk of most, is to leave the next heirs a house worth living in. She and her husband are a most private couple, and it was a while before they agreed to this book. I am grateful that they did, and I hope the book is above all a testament to Jane Northumberland and her restoration of the castle for future generations.

James McDonald

ABOVE Hogwarts scenes for the films *Harry Potter and the Chamber of Secrets* and *Harry Potter and the Philosopher's Stone* were filmed at Alnwick Castle – the flying lesson scene in the latter in the early medieval Inner Bailey pictured here. In 1650, Oliver Cromwell's forces imprisoned several thousand Scottish prisoners here for eight days, many of whom died.

THE STORY OF ALNWICK CASTLE AND THE PERCY FAMILY

EARLY HISTORY

The Percys' rise to the forefront of English feudal society began with William de Percy, who emigrated from France to England in 1066 or 1067 from the family's chief seat in Perci, in Normandy. Already wealthy, he was conveniently intimate with William the Conqueror.

The first draft of the Domesday Book shows that within twenty years of William the Conqueror invading England, William de Percy had become lord of over a hundred manors and settled as a magnate in both Yorkshire and Lincolnshire. While he and his descendants bore the title Baron Percy, they were not to own Alnwick Castle for another two hundred years. They did, however, acquire Petworth House in West Sussex in the twelfth century, which was probably then a manor.

Well before Alnwick Castle came into the equation the Percy name almost disappeared when William's grandson, another William, died without a male heir in 1175. The name was 'saved' by his daughter, Agnes de Percy, who married the well-connected Josceline de Louvain, a noble Dutchman from Brabant (now in Belgium) and the son of Godfrey I, Count of Louvain and Duke of Lower Lorraine, whose half-sister Queen Adeliza was married to the English King, Henry I. Despite these noble connections, Agnes's children were named Percy after her, not Louvain. Her son Richard Percy was one of the twenty-four barons who later made King John sign the Magna Carta.

Agnes's marriage to Josceline is alleged to have given the Percys the symbol of the blue lion reared up, technically called a lion rampant and cu, from her husband's armorial Louvain and Brabant bearings. The lion in lead on top of Syon House, the Duke and Duchess's London home, and its copy on the Lion Bridge by Alnwick Castle, can also be seen on the family silver, and on the crests of the full coat of arms of the Barons of Percy, and the Earls and Dukes of Northumberland. This lion statant is standing on all four legs; the Percy's has a straight tail.

Meanwhile another Norman baron, Ivo de Vesci, took over the Barony of Alnwick after Gilbert Tysen died at the Battle of Hastings during the Norman invasion and his descendant Eustace Fitz-John de Vesci is believed to have built Alnwick Castle in the early 1100s. Many other Norman motte-and-bailey castles appeared in the old Anglo-Saxon kingdom of Northumbria around this time. Although the south of England submitted quickly to Norman rule, resistance in the north continued for six years after 1066, especially in Northumbria, and we can assume that Alnwick Castle was built to ensure that the many rebellions in the north did not succeed.

OPPOSITE Ralph, the 12th Duke of Northumberland, on Alnwick Moor in Hulne Park. He descends by blood from Henry de Percy, who added the barony and castle of Alnwick to a vast inheritance in 1309.

ABOVE The Percy lion rampant azure, carved on the State Dining Room chimneypiece, is derived from the arms of Josceline de Louvain, son of Godfrey I of Brabant, who married the heiress Agnes de Percy in 1168 and took the Percy name. His half-sister married Henry I of England.

By the 1100s, the castle had a stone shell keep, which was the central fortress, protected by a deep ditch and curtain walls. All Norman castles were built like this and they did their job. In 1172 and in 1174, the castle was besieged by the Scottish King, William the Lion, without success and the King was infamously killed at Alnwick. The Keep is where the Percy family live today. The only way into its inner courtyard is via one gateway, which still has its Norman chevron design, with its zigzag mouldings, over the fine arch built by the de Vescis.

ABOVE The only way into the Keep's inner courtyard is via a gateway, which still has its Norman chevron zigzag design over the arch built by the de Vesci family in the early 1100s during the reigns of Henry I and II. The Percy family have now owned the castle for over 700 years.

THE FIRST BARONS PERCY OF ALNWICK

In 1295, over two hundred years after William the Conqueror died, the de Vesci line petered out, and the barony of Alnwick passed to the wealthy, extravagant but apparently chaste Bishop of Durham, Antony Bek. Bek was close to Edward I, who visited Alnwick many times. But despite being sent on missions for the King and fighting for him in the Battle of Falkirk, Bek had his lands confiscated, reinstated and confiscated again, because of a quarrel about Durham Cathedral. In 1309, two years after King Edward's death, Bek sold the Alnwick barony to Henry de Percy, for the vast sum of 10,000 marks. Thus he became **1st Baron Percy of Alnwick**. The current Duke still has the castle's 1309 title deeds, with a huge Edward II seal on them.

With Norman rule well established, Alnwick was still strategically important to England because it was so close to Scotland, and for hundreds of years the castle would be involved in battles against the independent Scots. The nobility, wealth, power and enduring influence in England of the Percy family over so many centuries is due, above all other reasons, to its ownership of land and this castle in Northumberland.

As a wealthy and loyal warrior, Henry de Percy, now 1st Baron Percy of Alnwick, must have seemed an ideal courtier to Edward I, and later to his unfortunate son, Edward II, who visited the castle. Henry also had a building gene in his blood, and extensivly repaired Alnwick Castle, adding corner towers. Despite many alternations since, you can see today its two rings of buildings in the classic motte-and-bailey design of the French invaders, which Henry inherited. The inner ring is the Keep and living quarters, set around an inner courtyard, accessed by its one gateway. This keep sits within a bailey, which is a technical name for a fortified walled enclosure. At Alnwick this is divided into two; the west side is the Outer Bailey and the east the Inner Bailey. Today these are two neat lawns, protected by the outer ring, a series of towers linked by high walls. As part of his upgrading of the castle's defensive features, Henry de Percy added the Abbot's, Postern, Constable's and Auditor's Towers, as well as part of the Ravine Tower.

Henry's son continued to add to the castle, and as **2nd Baron** built the imposing Octagonal Towers on the Keep over the chevron arches in 1350. The delightful carved figures ornamenting the battlements here were a fashion peculiar to Edward II's reign.

Alnwick is only 30 miles/48 kilometres or so from the Scottish border. Under the unstable rule of Edward II, the Scots' victory at the Battle of Bannockburn in 1314 allowed Scottish forces to raid unchecked throughout the north of England. The Percys' defensive fortifications were therefore opportune.

After Edward II was deposed and murdered, the long reign of his son, Edward III, from 1327 to 1377, suited Henry, the 2nd Baron, nicely. Edward III restored order after the disasters of his father's reign, relying on the nobility to fight for and with him. The Percy family kept in favour with him, fast becoming Northumberland's, and indeed England's, most powerful dynasty. Edward III paid Henry Percy, the 2nd Baron, 500 marks a year to lead an army. However, he effectively swapped this fee for Warkworth Castle and its lands, about 7 miles/ 11 kilometres from Alnwick and nearer the sea. Alnwick Castle is now considered grander, but Warkworth was apparently the family's preferred home. Henry died at Warkworth in 1352, possibly from the Black Death, which killed one-third of the English population at this time.

Henry's son, the **3rd Baron**, another Henry, succeeded. He also fought for Edward III, with the King's son, Edward the Black Prince, at the Battle of Crécy in France in 1346. The 3rd Baron Percy married Mary Lancaster, great-granddaughter of Henry III, who brought aspiring Lancaster blood into the veins of the Percy heirs. The 3rd Baron seems to have been at war most of his life, which left him little time for building. He died in 1368.

By the fourteenth century, the Percys were truly powerful and getting even more involved in politics. The next heir was the 4th Baron, another Henry, who also became the **1st Earl of Northumberland**. He and his brother, Thomas Percy, 1st Earl of Worcester, and Henry's son, named Sir Henry Percy but known as Harry Hotspur, appear to be the first Percys to oppose the monarch. This made life much more dangerous and few changes were made to the castle as a consequence.

The story of these Percys is legendary. Henry, the 4th Baron, was born at Alnwick Castle. After following Edward III loyally, when the King died he became Earl of Northumberland at the coronation of the ten-year-old Richard II in 1377. In 1381, the Percys' Northumberland power base was extended further, as they assumed ownership of another fortress, Prudhoe Castle, by marriage.

The 1st Earl's son Hotspur, born at Alnwick, acquired an early reputation as a great warrior, fighting against the Scots at the Battle of Otterburn in Northumberland in 1388 and again at the Battle of Humbleton Hill with his father in 1402. Hotspur is immortalized in Shakespeare's plays about Henry IV, in which his wife, Elizabeth, is represented as Kate, Lady Percy. Elizabeth, who was in the line of succession to the English throne, married Harry Hotspur when she was only about nine years old and Hotspur thirteen. Today on the wall of the Inner Bailey there is the Hotspur Seat, built by the 1st Duchess. Interestingly, Hotspur was the great-great-great-grandfather of Jane Seymour, wife of Henry VIII and mother of Edward VI.

Although Richard II made the 1st Earl a Marshal of England, he later suspected the Percys of treasonable plans. The 1st Earl switched his support to Richard's cousin, Bolingbroke, Duke of Lancaster, who deposed Richard and became Henry IV in 1399. Henry IV was the first King of England from the Lancaster branch of the Plantagenets, the other branch being the Yorks. He made the 1st Earl a Lord Constable of England and commander of the Royal Armies. Nevertheless, the 1st Earl's friendship with this monarch also turned sour.

As Shakespeare would later say in his plays, Henry IV was consumed with guilt for usurping his cousin and, despite the 1st Earl's victory over the Scots in 1402, Henry behaved badly to both him and to his son Hotspur, and owed the Percys money. In response, the 1st Earl and Hotspur organized two rebellions against the King. In the Battle of Shrewsbury in 1403, the gallant Hotspur was killed when he raised his visor to get some fresh air and was hit in the face by an arrow. On seeing Hotspur's body, Henry IV is said to have wept. But he so feared Hotspur's fame and popularity that he had his body cut up into four pieces and sent around England, including Newcastle, while his head was stuck on a pole in York. The pieces of Hotspur's body were finally delivered to his wife, Elizabeth, and buried in York Minster. He was then declared a traitor and the Crown confiscated his lands.

After Hotspur's death his father, the 1st Earl, was pardoned, but trouble continued and Alnwick Castle was repeatedly lost to and regained by royal forces. The 1st Earl's second rebellion led to his death in battle in 1408 and the castle was taken out of Percy hands.

Fortunately the next King, Henry V, was different from his father, Henry IV, and, wanting to lead a more united nation, made considerable reforms. As Prince of Wales, he had fought for his father against the 1st Earl and Hotspur, but when he became King, he pardoned Hotspur's son, Henry Northumberland, and in 1416 returned the earldom and Alnwick Castle to him. Indeed the King pardoned most of England's nobility at this time. He had got to know the **2nd Earl** when as youths they had both lived at Windsor. Later he made him General of the Marches, and awarded him a prestigious and grand military role, making him responsible for the northern borders of England.

Nonetheless, peace continued to elude the Percys. The King died, aged thirty-six, in France in 1422 and the occasionally mad Henry VI succeeded him. In the winter of 1424, a Scottish raiding party burned much of Alnwick town, although the castle survived intact.

Worse was to come with the War of the Roses, the long dynastic civil war for the English throne fought between the two rival branches of the royal house of Plantagenet: the houses of 'red rose' Lancaster and 'white rose' York. The Percys sided with the Lancastrians, led by Henry VI, and the 2nd Earl was killed at the first Battle of St Albans in 1455.

Five years later Henry VI was captured and Edward of York became King, as Edward IV. On the death of his father in the War of the Roses, Henry Northumberland had become **3rd Earl**, and he did not support the Yorkist Edward IV. But only six years later, he too was killed, at the Battle of Townton in 1461; he was forty years old. The battle was a decisive defeat for the Lancastrians and probably the bloodiest ever fought on English soil: 38,000 men were killed in an orgy of bloodletting, either in a rain of arrows or in gory hand-to-hand fighting. Alnwick Castle and all the 3rd Earl's estates were confiscated and his son Henry, the 4th Earl, was imprisoned in the Tower of London.

The 4th Earl's legacy is the Barbican at Alnwick Castle. This is the grand fortified gatehouse that, when you enter from Alnwick town, is the main entrance into the castle compound. At the time it probably had a drawbridge over a moat. It was finished in 1475 and the 4th Earl's shield, containing the lion of Josceline de Louvain, is on the front. The current Duke's grandfather called it one of the finest examples of fifteenth-century medieval architecture in Britain.

During the War of the Roses the castle was taken, regained and taken again. Facing rebellion from his own supporters, the King countered by letting the 4th Earl, Henry, out of the Tower of London and restored the earldom to him in 1473, also giving him back Alnwick Castle. Not surprisingly, Henry became a Yorkist supporter, fighting with Edward IV, and he was highly popular in the north of England too. But in 1483 only ten years after Henry was remade an earl, Edward IV died and the throne went to Richard III.

The 4th Earl supported the new King, but only up to a point. Richard III was killed two years later in the Battle of Bosworth Field against the Lancastrian Henry Tudor. Richard was the last Yorkist king, the last of the Plantagenet dynasty and the last English king to be killed in battle. His death was made inevitable by the actions of the 4th Earl, who in the midst of the battle held back his troops, thus abandoning Richard III to his fate. The 4th Earl in effect paid for this four years later when he was murdered by a mob who were enraged at his overzealous tax collections.

He was succeeded by his eleven-year-old son, Henry Algernon, in 1489, by which time the Tudor dynasty had begun. The Scots and the English were to continue fighting for some time. But the **5th Earl** preferred the life of the Renaissance court to warfare. Cultured and terribly extravagant, he loved magnificence and display, and enjoyed the honour of waiting on the King of France at the Field of the Cloth of Gold.

Luckily for us, the 5th Earl kept the 1512 Northumberland Household Book. Despite his court duties, he travelled between his castles, and had a staff of 166 and enough provisions to feed an additional 57 people each day. Between them all they drank 40 gallons (320 pints) of beer and 4 gallons of wine (about 24 bottles) a day. It also records that his furniture, even including the glass for the windows, was carried about with the Earl from one residence to another.

Unlike his predecessors, who had all been killed, the 5th Earl died peacefully, in 1527.

Henry, the **6th Earl** of Northumberland, was twenty-five years old when he inherited. Known as 'the Unthrifty' and tragically romantic, he does not appear to have done much at Alnwick except repair it. His life was unhappy: he seemed to be a victim of life, enduring much grief caused by Henry VIII, as well as from his wife and family. He was also often ill with ague, a feverish condition similar to malaria.

Before he became Earl, the youthful Lord Percy was an aide to Cardinal Wolsey. Often at court, he passed the time in the Queen's quarters, flirting with the ladies-in-waiting, especially Anne Boleyn. Henry Percy and Anne reputedly fell in love with each other, probably around 1523. However, when their love affair became public they were forbidden to marry because the Cardinal thought that Anne's family was inferior, saying (as George Cavendish, his gentleman-usher, recorded):

> I am amazed at your foolishness in getting entangled, even engaged, to this silly girl at court – I mean Anne Boleyn. Have you not considered your position? After the death of your noble father you stand to inherit one of the greatest earldoms in the country. It would thus have been more proper if you had sought the consent of your father in this affair and to have made his highness the King privy to it, requesting his royal blessing. Had you done so, he would not only have

welcomed your request but would, I can assure you, have promoted you to a position more suited to your noble estate . . . But now look what you have done by your thoughtlessness. You have not only offended your own father but also your sovereign and pledged yourself to someone whom neither would agree to be suitable.

The young lovers were forced to separate, and Henry Percy is said to have sent a note to Anne begging her never to love anyone else. She subsequently married Henry VIII.

In the meantime Henry Percy was forced to marry the older Mary Talbot, daughter of the Earl of Shrewsbury. The marriage was unhappy and childless, and later Mary sought a divorce.

In 1530 Henry VIII ordered Henry Percy to arrest the Catholic Cardinal Wolsey, as recorded in Shakespeare's play *Henry VIII*. When the King wanted to get rid of his wife Anne, he accused Percy of adultery with her and had him interrogated. Percy survived that ordeal, but the King asked him to sit on the jury that found Anne guilty of adultery with someone else. When the guilty verdict was announced, Percy collapsed and had to be carried from the courtroom.

The Percys, who were then Catholics, suffered further turmoil when Henry VIII faced rebellion in the north of England over his dissolution of the monasteries, which included the Hulne Priory in Alnwick Castle's park. Thomas Percy, brother of the 6th Earl, was executed for his role in the Catholic rebellion known as the Pilgrimage of Grace in 1536.

The 6th Earl died a year later, in 1537, without any children, in poverty and in debt. On the day he died, Richard Layton visited and found him '*languens in extremis*, sight and speech failed, his stomach swollen so great as I never see none, and his whole body as yellow as saffron'. The dying Earl left his estates to Henry VIII on condition that, or in the hope that, one day the family would be forgiven and their status restored. Anne Boleyn's personal prayer book is today in the castle's library. For twenty years, Alnwick Castle continued to be used by the King's minions for its historic role as a base for the defence of the north-east of England and for incursions into Scotland.

Percy fortunes changed on the death of Henry VIII, when his eldest, and Catholic, daughter Mary became Queen in 1547. In 1552 she restored the earldom to Thomas, son of the executed Thomas Percy and nephew of the 6th Earl. Known as the 'Blessed' Thomas, the **7th Earl** was a devout Catholic.

When Queen Mary's half-sister and Anne Boleyn's daughter,

Elizabeth I, succeeded as Queen, Thomas remained in favour, but not for long. Soon out of favour for his Catholicism, he stripped Alnwick Castle of all its furniture to make it uninhabitable for his rivals and Elizabeth I's favourites in the north of England, saying it was 'utterly unfurnished and [had] not so much as one bed in it'. But five years later, in 1567, he apparently felt more secure and had moved back in.

By this time, the castle had stopped serving any military purpose and the moat was filled in. The glass in the windows suffered so much from 'extreame wind' that it was taken down and stored when the Earl was not in residence; one imagines that the estate officials who lived in the castle permanently were in the winter often freezing as a consequence. Thomas carried out some restorations, as apparently the castle was in a bad state of repair, but his Catholic loyalties intervened. The English Catholic Rising of the North in 1569 against Elizabeth I in support of her cousin Mary, Queen of Scots, was organized in part from both Alnwick Castle and the Percys' nearby Warkworth Castle.

This uprising was a disaster for the Percy family. Alnwick Castle was forced to surrender to Elizabeth I's Protestant forces. Thomas, the 7th Earl, was captured in Scotland and eventually beheaded in 1572, aged forty-four. He is considered a martyr by the Church of Rome for refusing to give up his faith to save his life; Pope Leo XIII beatified him in 1895. On his death, Elizabeth I's servants pillaged both Alnwick and Warkworth Castles.

The 7th Earl and his wife did not have any children either, so in 1572 the earldom went to Thomas's brother, Henry Percy, who became the **8th Earl**. But he too was alleged to be a Catholic and Elizabeth I had him imprisoned in the Tower of London, where he died, in mysterious circumstances, in 1585.

On his death his twenty-one-year-old son Henry became the **9th Earl**. He was known as the 'Wizard Earl'. After the folly of his father and uncle, one would have hoped that this young nobleman would restore Percy fortunes. He was based in the south to be near court but his cousin Thomas Percy made dramatic improvements to the castle's estate to increase revenue, dealing with the attendant problems of an absentee landlord. The 9th Earl was incredibly bright, creating one of the finest libraries of his day, on topics that included military tactics, navigation, astronomy, alchemy and cartography. He was also a friend of Sir Walter Raleigh, addicted to smoking tobacco, and by 1591 had potatoes from America on the menu.

When Elizabeth I died in 1603 and there was doubt as to

who would succeed her, the 9th Earl was a great supporter of James VI of Scotland, who became King of England and Ireland as James I. But the 9th Earl's consequent rising wealth and influence were halted by another disaster.

On 4 November 1605, he dined at Syon House with his cousin Thomas Percy, who held the post of Constable of Alnwick Castle. The next day Guy Fawkes was discovered trying to blow up the Houses of Parliament in what became known as the Gunpowder Plot. Thomas Percy was one of the principal plotters and was later shot dead trying to make his escape. Apparently, Thomas was disappointed with the King's lack of tolerance towards the Catholics, being one himself. Besides providing the plotters with money, he also secured the lease for the vault underneath the House of Lords where thirty-six barrels of gunpowder were found under coal and wood faggots.

Suspicion immediately fell on the 9th Earl, and although he claimed innocence, he was arrested and imprisoned in the Tower of London. He was held there for fifteen years and only released after paying a colossal fine of £30,000. Thereafter, he was banished to his estate at Petworth, dying in 1632.

For 118 years, the influence of the Percy family in the north of England waned until the middle of the eighteenth century.

Algernon, the **10th Earl**, was thirty years old when he succeeded in 1632. He remained in the south of England most of his life, living largely at Syon House and Petworth. He was a collector of Old Masters and a friend and patron of Van Dyck, and founded the Percy picture collection in the late 1630s.

Algernon's marriage to Elizabeth Howard brought with it Northumberland House in central London. This grand house took up most of the land between Northumberland Avenue and Whitehall, backing on to Great Scotland Yard. Had it not later been demolished, it would now stand close to Trafalgar Square today.

Algernon was to display the independence of mind that defines the house of Percy, but conscious of his father's and grandfather's imprisonments, he learned to be judicious in his behaviour. He seemed to be in favour with the King, Charles I, and in 1637 he became Lord High Admiral of England and President of the Council of War. However, he also served in both the House of Commons and later the House of Lords, and when the country became convulsed by civil war was the highest-ranking member of Charles I's government to take the side of Parliament. Though he supported the 'constitutional cause', his independent attitude in seeking a compromise between King and Parliament, together with the widespread respect that he commanded and his great influence, ensured that, overall, his vast estates emerged from the conflict intact.

This was no mean feat. He was made Governor of the Royal Children, who lived at Syon House, was deeply opposed to the execution of Charles I and refused to take part in the republican 'Commonwealth' led by Oliver Cromwell, despite Cromwell's requests. While he supported the restoration of the monarchy after Cromwell's death in 1658, he opposed Charles II's policy of revenge after his coronation and voted against the bill to execute the fifty-nine commissioners who had signed the death warrant of Charles I in 1649.

Meanwhile, matters at Alnwick Castle reached their lowest point ever in its history. During the Civil War the castle had been invaded by Scottish armies, and then captured first by Royalists and then by Parliamentarians. The 10th Earl's property, including the castle, was severely damaged, as was Alnwick town. The chaos caused by the Parliamentarians also meant it was impossible to collect rents and the 10th Earl had to sell off many of his fine paintings and silver.

Oliver Cromwell and his forces inflicted the greatest horror. In 1650 he captured 9,000 Scottish prisoners at the Battle of Dunbar, and took about half of them to the castle, where they were imprisoned in one of the baileys without food or water. Many died of abuse and sickness. The rest were marched to Durham, over 50 miles/80 kilometres south, and only 1,400 survived. Several suits of armour of these despicable English republicans now decorate the Private Staircase in the castle.

When Algernon died of old age at his Petworth estate in 1668, his 24-year-old son Josceline became the **11th Earl**. Josceline's marriage to Lady Elizabeth Wriothesley, the daughter of the Earl of Southampton, produced a son called Henry and a daughter called Elizabeth. There is little to say about Henry, as he died when he was a baby. Then in 1670, when Elizabeth was only four years old, her father died in Turin on a Grand Tour and the Percys suddenly found themselves without a male heir.

Josceline's wife, the Countess of Northumberland, was in Paris when her husband died. As a young and very eligible widow, she went on to marry the 1st Duke of Montagu. She must have been pleased if not complicit in ensuring that her very young daughter Elizabeth Percy inherited the vast Percy and Northumberland estates. Two of the 11th Earl's older brothers died early, and the other brother, apart from being exiled in disgrace, never married. Only one of his two sisters had a child but he, Algernon Sydney, was a republican in exile in France and later beheaded.

Elizabeth had two catastrophic marriages when she was barely of age; one husband died and one was murdered. At the age of fifteen she married her third husband, the 6th Duke of Somerset, Charles Seymour, in 1682. They fixed up Alnwick Castle a little, but the Duke focused all the Percy money on improving Petworth House, where they lived in considerable grandeur.

Elizabeth was known as **Baroness Percy, Duchess of Somerset**, and was Mistress of the Robes to Queen Anne. Her husband, Charles, was known as the 'Proud Duke' and was by all accounts a difficult man. He was also a snob, who liked pomp; Macaulay called him 'a man in whom the pride of birth and rank amounted almost to a disease'.

Charles and Elizabeth's only son was born in 1684 and named Algernon; he later became the 7th Duke of Somerset, and after his marriage to Frances Thynne he gave his parents two grandchildren, George, Lord Beauchamp, and Lady Elizabeth Seymour. Born in 1716, the great-granddaughter of Josceline, 11th Earl of Northumberland, Lady Elizabeth Seymour is critical to the story of the Percy family, for she was to become eventually the 1st Duchess of Northumberland. It is the story of these three generations – grandparents, son and grandchildren – that resulted in the 1066 Percy bloodline being once again preserved through Percy women, the re-creation of the earldom and the creation of the dukedom of Northumberland.

Lady Elizabeth Seymour visited Alnwick Castle each summer with her brother and parents in the 1730s. While neither an intellectual nor a great beauty, she knew her family history and that she was, despite being a daughter, due a reasonable inheritance. Her grandfather, the 6th Duke of Somerset, apparently loathed his daughter-in-law, and perhaps his son, but assumed that his grandson, Elizabeth's brother George, Lord Beauchamp, would eventually inherit everything, including Alnwick Castle, as a Duke of Somerset.

When Lady Elizabeth Seymour met the dashing Sir Hugh Smithson, 4th Baronet, and he proposed marriage, she wrote to her parents saying she was 'flabbergasted' to have such a suitor and, clearly in love, admitted 'a partiality for him'. However, although she had no other suitors and was getting to an age when she had better marry quickly, her parents were deeply reluctant to give their consent. Sir Hugh was considered extremely popular in society and had an income of £4,000 a year, but although he inherited the title of 4th Baronet his great-grandfather was originally a haberdasher. In those days, when people were obsessed with lineage and

nobility to a degree we cannot quite imagine today, this was a black mark. But when Elizabeth's parents banned her from contact with Sir Hugh, she apparently made herself ill from heartache and they reluctantly agreed to the marriage. Nonetheless, it took another year of negotiation. The marriage was eventually settled by the clever moves of Sir Hugh in winning over Elizabeth's old and cantankerous grandfather, the 'Proud' 6th Duke of Somerset.

Elizabeth and Sir Hugh married in 1740. Living happily at Sir Hugh's Palladian house Stanwick Hall in Stanwick Park in Yorkshire, their world changed in 1744 when Elizabeth's brother George died in Italy on his Grand Tour. The old 6th Duke was livid and blamed his son, George's father, saying George's death was 'a judgment upon him for all his undutiful-ness'.

Knowing that Elizabeth was now sole heiress to the Percy estates, and not in favour of her, the old Duke spitefully asked George II to revive and give him the title of Earl of Northumberland with a clause, called a remainder, that ensured that on his death everything, including Alnwick Castle, would go to his daughter's son, Charles Wyndham, rather than his eldest son's daughter, Lady Elizabeth Seymour. This was an important moment in Percy history. When Algernon and his wife, Frances, their son having just died, heard that their only daughter was about to be disinherited from the Percy fortune, frantic negotiations with George II ensued. Algernon sent his confident and impressive son-in-law, Sir Hugh Smithson, to see the King face to face. Born in Hanover as the son of the Prince of Brunswick-Lüneburg Althand (later George I), George II was by all accounts fascinated by the grand names of the English nobility – and especially the proud house of Percy. At this meeting with the King, Sir Hugh succeeded in saving his wife's inheritance, so foiling her grandfather.

As a result, when the 'Proud' Duke died in 1748 Algernon became the **7th Duke of Somerset** and the King, by letters patent, revived the earldom, so he also became **1st Earl of Northumberland**. A remainder ensured that on Algernon's death the earldom would pass to his daughter Elizabeth and, by her marriage, to Sir Hugh.

THE 1ST DUKE AND DUCHESS

When her father died in 1750 Elizabeth became Baroness Percy, while her husband became the Earl of Northumberland. She inherited Alnwick Castle and most of the other Percy estates except Petworth House, which was left to her cousin, Charles Wyndham, 2nd Earl of Egremont, and she brought the family back to live at Alnwick.

Elizabeth was Lady of the Bedchamber to Queen Charlotte; she travelled extensively around Europe; she was entertained by Louis XVI at Versailles; and she shopped, amassing a vast collection of objects and works of art ranging from paintings, ivories, gems, coins and prints to shells, marbles, wood carvings and curiosities of all sorts. A colourful character, she also kept a diary, which adds a feminine note to the male-dominated story of the Percy family.

When Elizabeth's husband, Hugh, became the Earl of Northumberland, he dropped his family name of Smithson and became a Percy by Act of Parliament. Life became only better for the talented and ambitious Hugh. It is said that he was proposed as Lord Chamberlain, but that when the Marquis of Hertford was appointed instead, the 28-year-old George III, known as 'Mad George', conferred a dukedom on Hugh in 1766 in apparent. In this way he became the **1st Duke of Northumberland** and Elizabeth the **1st Duchess**. A limitation stipulated that any children of Hugh's Percy wife could inherit the titles of earl and duke but if he remarried and had children from a second wife, they would not be allowed to inherit the title of earl or duke.

In 1753, he became Lord of the Bedchamber to George II; then, on the accession of George III, he became Lord Chamberlain to Queen Charlotte, and later Lord Lieutenant of Middlesex, then of Northumberland and from 1763 of Ireland ,and Master of the Horse in 1778. In 1784 he was created Lord Lovaine and Baron Alnwick, and it was stated that these later titles were to be inherited by his second son. He was also a Knight of the Garter and Vice-Admiral of Northumberland and America.

By all accounts, this Duke and Duchess had a strong marriage, despite each having their own peccadilloes. Hugh was reputedly 'an unusually handsome man', highly intelligent and with a magnetic personality, and as we know, Elizabeth married him for love. Though his marriage had been highly advantageous for Hugh, he and his wife were in love with each other throughout their lives. In her diary for 1763, she recorded that her husband included in his speech a 'vast compliment' to her, and 'was the first man that ever brought a declaration of love into a speech in Parliament'. Nevertheless, the 1st Duke had many affairs, the most notable being with Elizabeth Macie, who in 1765 gave birth to his illegitimate son, James Smithson. When James died in 1836, he left his fortune to a nephew who, having no heirs, left it to the US government to establish a foundation 'for the increase and diffusion of knowledge among men', which, on being established in Washington, is now known as the Smithsonian Institute.

Abiding by her principle that 'we forgive as long as we love', the Duchess had her own lovers too. She wrote about them in her diary using numbers: 'nine not so prudent as usual' or 'caught out with 500 on the stairs by Princess Augusta' and so on. Heather Ewing observes in her book *The Lost World of James Smithson* that it seems that the Duchess knew about the Duke's affair with Elizabeth Macie, for when she had to leave the Duke in Bath with his mistress in December 1761, though she rarely mentioned personal pain she wrote, 'Left Bath quite alone – shocking Day.'

The Percy–Seymour–Smithson union between Hugh and Elizabeth produced a daughter and no fewer than two lines of peers: Hugh Percy (1742–1817), who became the 2nd Duke of Northumberland, and Algernon Percy (1750–1830), later known as Lord Lovaine and the 1st Earl of Beverley, whose heirs would inherit the dukedom with the accession of the 5th Duke, George Percy, in 1865.

This elite, rich, ambitious and energetic couple were to greatly influence British eighteenth-century patronage of the arts with their wide-ranging taste. Horace Walpole reported in a letter of 1752 that the extravagant Earl and Countess 'are building at Northumberland House, at Syon, at Stanwick, at Alnwick and Warkworth Castles'. However, Elizabeth's greatest achievement was probably the restoration of her beloved Alnwick Castle, which from 1750 was to enter its golden age.

On their first visit after her inheritance, in 1751, the castle was so dilapidated that she and Hugh had to sleep in the old exchequer house next to the gatehouse. Yet she and her husband soon breathed new life into it and the area, restoring not only the castle but also the surrounding parks and estates, all their efforts being recorded in her diaries as 'works order'd at Alnwick'. The current Duke says of their work: 'The 1st Duke was a great agriculturalist and he revolutionized farming up here; it was the agricultural revolution, timing was good and so he could increase the rents and the income from his own

Most of the towers forming the keep, which had consisted of independent lodgings connected with one another by curtain walls, were rebuilt, some of them in a different position, and connected with one another by passages, space for which was found by taking in a strip from the Inner Ward. The old banqueting hall remained the dining room, the medieval kitchens became drawing rooms, and the western side of the keep was converted into a series of state bedrooms. The southern side was converted into quarters for the Duke and Duchess in the Octagonal Towers, while over the archway was a room called the breakfast room. The main entrance to the keep was at the north-western side of the Inner Ward, leading to a magnificent fan-shaped staircase, which ascended to the suite of drawing rooms.

A number of buildings in the Inner and Outer Baileys were removed in 1755. The outer walls of the castle and towers, which had become ruinous, were restored. The Avener's Tower was rebuilt and the tower that currently houses the clock was built for water. Later in the 1770s, a house between two square battlemented towers was removed so that an arch could be constructed leading to what is now the Alnwick Garden. Other towers were rebuilt and stabling was created outside the Outer Bailey wall around a square courtyard where the shop and café are now located.

Wherever possible the rooms were decorated in a mass of Gothic tracery and stucco, and the family coat of arms and ancient emblems were placed all over this. Large windows were installed for better views outdoors. The architect James Paine was employed to install a grand, bold and curvaceous elliptical staircase in 1764.

Despite the changes, overall the exterior antiquity of the medieval castle remained, but there was a plethora of Gothic windows ('totally out of keeping with a medieval Castle', according to Duke Alan Ian) and fancy bits on the battlements. A stonemason spent twenty years carving medieval-style, life-sized statues for the towers, roofs and battlements in the fashion popular during the fourteenth century.

Once Robert Adam had restored Syon House in 1769, Elizabeth replaced James Paine and had Robert Adam sent up to Alnwick to finish off her Gothic rooms with more fan vaulting, stucco tracery and a profusion of heraldic ornament.

The new interiors were a riot of colour, none of which were quite medieval, but that was not the intention, for they

enterprises.' While Alnwick was for them one of a number of houses, the current Duke says: 'I think it was an important centre of their lives. Through Alnwick they wanted to go back to the Percy roots.'

Since her marriage Elizabeth had taken to studying a number of subjects, including architecture. Having greatly admired Horace Walpole's Strawberry Hill house in Surrey, designed in the new Gothic style by the architect Robert Adam, saying in her diaries that she 'never saw anything half so pretty', in the 1750s she initiated a grand rebuilding of Alnwick Castle in the Gothic style.

Elizabeth's modifications, which started in the 1750s and were finished in the early 1770s, included a new dining room, breakfast room, saloon, drawing room, library, chapel, state bedchambers and dressing rooms. The 8th Duke, Alan Ian, describes in his 1920s guide to the castle how the castle changed at this time:

ABOVE A pair of 1760s portraits of the 1st Duke and Duchess, attributed to Francis Lindo, dominate the State Dining Room, honouring their restoration of the castle and estate in the 1750s and 1760s.

were designed to please the Duchess. The ceiling of the Great Drawing Room was pink and green, and the Saloon had blue walls with white trelliswork in stucco. As well as using English cabinet-makers such as Chippendale, Walle and Reilly, she introduced French pieces, including huge mirrors. The stools along the Warkworth Corridor are of Adam's Gothic design, as are the carved lectern and armchair in the Chapel.

The work at Alnwick received mixed reviews. In 1775 F. Grose, in *The Antiquities of England and Wales*, called the restoration 'one of the most magnificent models of a great baronial castle'. Elizabeth Montagu, visiting in 1772, called the castle 'the most noble Gothick building imagineable'. And James Plumptre in his 1790s *Journals of a Tourist* called the Library the largest and most 'handsome room . . . in which the Family generally reside'. Eileen Harris, in her book *The Genius of Robert Adam*, says that 'few private places of worship in England could vie with the colourful, glittering magnificence of the chapel', built at vast expense.

However, she reports that James Plumptre was filled with such indignation on seeing the chapel that he left the castle after seeing 'the House of prayers turned into the House of ostentation of the Percy family'.

It is a great shame that we cannot see the 1st Duchess's Gothic interiors for ourselves, as they were later destroyed by her grandson; we can only see Adam's drawings for them at the Soane Museum in London.

ABOVE Alnwick Castle by Canaletto in 1752, showing its condition before the Percy heiress Lady Elizabeth Seymour, later 1st Duchess, restored it in her favourite Gothic style, employing James Paine and then Robert Adam. The current Duke doubts that Canaletto ever came to the castle, saying the painting is out of perspective, particularly the figures on the hillside.
OPPOSITE The 1st Duchess was an inveterate traveller and collector of art and all sorts of objects. Her ivory relief of *The Judgement of Paris*, which hangs in the Ante-Library, shows Paris of Troy giving the apple to Aphrodite, as she promised him Helen, the wife of the King of Sparta. Sparta's revenge led to the Trojan War and the fall of Troy.

Nonetheless, it appears that the designs reflected her vibrant character and her lifestyle. Her entertainments were legendary for their splendour and extravagance. Horace Walpole, without much gallantry, called her 'a jovial heap of contradictions . . . her person was more vulgar than anything but her conversation, which was larded indiscriminately with stories of her ancestors and her footmen'. He also said that 'Show, and crowds, and junketing, were her endless pursuits'; happy to accept an invitation from her, despite the snippiness of his comments, he noted at Northumberland House in 1762 'a pompous festivo; not only the whole house, but the whole garden was illuminated'. She often sent off hundreds of invitations and then forgot how many people she had asked verbally, and over six hundred people would arrive for a soirée. For George III's birthday in 1764, she invited 1,500 people to a party which the *London Chronicle* reported was 'conducted with a decorum and magnificence peculiar to the Countess of Northumberland', noting the 'astonishing degree of splendour' inside. James Boswell recorded that the Duke and Duchess 'live in a most princely manner . . . yet they are easy and affable'. Her candle bill alone was reported to be £400 a year – a colossal sum in those days.

The Duchess's sense of fun, largesse and theatre extended to her wardrobe. In the heat of summer, her mother commented with some humour on Elizabeth's heavy finery, 'she in silver stuff of four pounds a yard'. Walpole was typically more scathing, reporting seeing her at a masquerade that she had 'a pyramid of baubles upon her head' and in Paris, 'her belly all diamonds'. On another occasion the Duchess of Richmond wrote that Elizabeth's dress 'was made of silver ground with velvet flowers of all colours; it look'd like an Old Bed'.

Walpole also recorded that the Duchess 'was mischievous under the appearance of frankness; generous and friendly without delicacy or sentiment'. Certainly her diaries and notebooks are frank, but they are often highly amusing, lack malice and reveal a kind nature, along with an affability and great cheerfulness in her hard work as chatelaine.

What is extraordinary, and curious, about the 1st Duchess's life is the huge amount of time she spent abroad, away from her husband. Unlike many Grand Tourists of the time, she went to Italy only once, with her husband in 1773, but she made countless trips to France, Germany, Switzerland and Holland, the latter the homeland of her ancestor Josceline de Louvain of Brabant, who, as noted earlier, also took the name of Percy from his wife as Elizabeth's husband had done.

On these tours the Duchess greatly added to the Percy art collection, displaying a highly shrewd, disciplined and

organized character. While her husband was more classical in his tastes, the Duchess preferred Dutch and Flemish paintings. You will see some of her acquisitions later in this book. Her own 'List' of her paintings made in 1772 reveals a leaning towards 'low life' scenes of ordinary people, which she acquired along with prints, ivories, coins, medals, china and other *objets d'art*.

She travelled in great state across Europe, putting all her art purchases in a wagon, while she sat up front in her coach, always with her dog Tizzy, followed by a vast retinue of servants. She suffered from gout and gallstones, especially later in life, but this did not put her off. At a picnic in Geneva she was surrounded by beggars 'all covr'd with Rags & Lice'. When she asked her servants to give them food there was such a mad scramble that, trapped in her chair, she was almost pushed 'to the Ground' in the mayhem and a beggar fell on top of her. Indeed her sharp and humorous observations of detail at all social levels – whether in an Emperor's court or an inn – her energetic determination to see everything, her forthrightness and confidence, and her records of the cost of everything, make her journals a gem of the eighteenth century.

On her first trip to the Netherlands in 1766, she toured significant art collections, including that of Jan de Bisschop in Rotterdam, whose curiosities were 'stuffed into a house not larger than a Middle Sized Closet'. She also visited another important collector, Brammcamp; but highly confident of her own opinion, on inspecting his vast collection she claimed he 'had not the least taste for pictures'. She returned to the Netherlands in 1767 and 1769 more determined to make purchases, buying, for example, *Interior with a Lady at her Toilet* by Anthonie Palamedesz. She visited a fourth time in 1771, each time driving a hard bargain in her purchases.

During these visits abroad, she made an important collection of ivories, some of which are on view today in the Drawing Room. Most of the ivories are decorated with Low Country peasant scenes of merry-making in the seventeenth-century Dutch style, after Teniers and Ostade, and fanciful hunting scenes after Philips Wouwerman, another celebrated seventeenth-century Dutch painter.

Anne French, in her book *Art Treasures in the North: Northern Families on the Grand Tour*, singles out *The Gorge at Tivoli* by Marlow as one of the Duchess's 'exceptional' purchases. She also writes that the Duchess's patronage of Pompeo Batoni, and of William Marlow, helps illustrate that she was a major patron in the eighteenth century and that her eight *veduta* paintings (*veduta* is Italian for a view) – vistas of Tivoli, Ariccia and the Bay of Naples – are particularly fine. Some of what remains of her paintings hang at Syon House, but a handful, such as the Breughel in the Private Dining Room, hang around the castle.

While the Duke and Duchess shared some similar artistic tastes, the Duke made his own collection. His more classical tastes were influenced by his Grand Tour in 1733, when he visited Rome, Venice, Vicenza and Milan. When Canaletto arrived in London in 1746, he commissioned him to paint *London Seen Through an Arch of Westminster Bridge*, making him one of the artist's earliest English patrons. Today it is on show in the Upper Guard Chamber. Two more Venetian street views by Canaletto are in the Saloon, along with a painting of Northumberland House and Alnwick Castle. Canaletto's painting of Syon is in the Upper Guard Chamber. As well as Canalettos, the 1st Duke collected classical art and supported Giles Hussey in Italy.

The Duchess became ill and died in 1776, aged sixty. Her funeral in Westminster Abbey was filled with a crowd so large that the pallbearers could hardly get the coffin down the aisle. Clambering for a view, crowds climbed up on to the ancient stonework screen between the St Nicholas and St Edmund Chapels, which then collapsed, injuring many people and further delaying the service, which eventually continued, notwithstanding the moans of the injured.

After the Duchess's death, the Duke erected monuments to her memory on the estate, including a tower at Brizlee, an observatory at Ratcheugh and a picnic house next to the Great Tower at Hulne Priory (see page 227), which had been some of her favourite destinations for carriage rides. The Duke died twelve years after his wife in 1786.

THE 2ND AND 3RD DUKES

As Earl Percy the Duke and Duchess's son Hugh became Baron of six baronies on his mother's death in 1776 and the **2nd Duke** on his father's in 1786. Unlike his friend the Prince Regent, later George IV, who started work on the Brighton Pavilion in 1787, the 2nd Duke did not carry out much building in the Keep at Alnwick, as his parents had only recently restored it. He did, however, build the Estate Offices.

As a youth, he travelled a great deal to Gibraltar, Naples, Istanbul and America, despite suffering from ill health throughout his life. It is said that before he became Duke he had consumption, a form of tuberculosis, but his 1761 Grand Tour cured him. As his mother took Tizzy, so he took with him on his tour his Spitzbergen dog.

He married twice. His first wife, whom he married in 1764, was the daughter of the 3rd Earl of Bute. In 1779 they divorced and he married Frances Julia Burrell. Oddly enough, Frances's older sister Isabella married the 2nd Duke's brother Algernon, 1st Earl of Beverley. Isabella was the mother of George, who became the 5th Duke in the nineteenth century. The 2nd Duke and his second wife had nine children.

Hugh was a military man, having served as a young man in the Seven Years War, as ADC to George III and as a colonel in the American War of Independence, notably at the skirmish at Lexington, where his actions probably saved the British forces from disaster. While in America, Hugh met the native American Iroquois leader Thayandanegea, whose portrait by the artist Gilbert Stuart is on display at Syon House, along with one of the Duke's children. His other notable contribution to the family's art collection include commissions from, for example, the artist Thomas Philips, who was sent to Paris during the Peace of Amiens in 1802 to paint Napoleon. This now hangs on the private staircase at Alnwick.

Earlier on their Grand Tours Hugh and his brother were painted by the fashionable artist Pompeo Batoni; the 2nd Duke's portrait is particularly fine. He also had painted a typical Grand Tour portrait by Nathaniel Dance. In this the young lord is sitting down against the backdrop of Rome, and gazing into the distance, while his tutor stands by, apparently lecturing him. The scene appears to be in the gardens of the Villa Borghese, with its famous Borghese vase, now in the Louvre. It is not evident from the paintings, but contemporary accounts said that in addition to suffering from gout and poor eyesight, the 2nd Duke was unattractive, too thin, and had a large nose. Accounts of his character are more flattering, saying that he was honourable, candid, decent, impeccably mannered and immensely generous with his wealth. A portrait of him in old age is in the Burgundy Bedroom.

The 2nd Duke created the Percy Tenantry Volunteers in case Napoleon invaded England's north-east coast. They never numbered more than 1,500 men, so would have been useless against massive French forces, but the Duke trained them in the guerrilla tactics that had been used against him in America. The display of weapons at the castle entrance, in the Lower Guard Chamber, belonged to these volunteers.

The Napoleonic Wars left the English economy floundering and Hugh responded by lowering rents, which made him popular in Alnwick throughout his time as Duke. He was also popular with the ladies, if we are to believe the diaries of his friend Casanova, with whom he shared a mistress called Liselle, who was a ballerina.

Hugh is buried in the Percy vault of the Chapel of St Nicholas in Westminster Abbey, where twenty-nine members of the family are buried, the first being the 1st Duchess's brother in 1744 and the most recent the 10th Duke (the present Duke's father) in 1988.

On the death of the 2nd Duke in 1817, his son, another Hugh, became the **3rd Duke**. He held the title for exactly the same number of years as his father – thirty. He married Lady Charlotte Florentia Clive, who was the daughter of Edward Clive, 1st Earl of Powis, son of the hugely wealthy 'Clive of India'. Her portrait by Thomas Lawrence, a prominent Regency painter, can be seen in the State Dining Room.

The 3rd Duke and Duchess were at the forefront of British aristocratic society in the first half of the nineteenth century and lived mostly in Northumberland House, in London, or on their Syon estate. Even so, the Duke made sure that the new east coast railway was not built too near the castle. They bought a great deal of furniture and silver gilt, but their greatest contribution, now at Alnwick, appears to be the two Cucci cabinets made for Louis XIV of France, which they bought at an auction for Northumberland House, and which are probably the most expensive pieces of Baroque furniture in the world. You can see them in the Drawing Room (pages 78–9).

The 3rd Duke was chosen to be the Ambassador to France and representative of George IV at the coronation of Charles X of France in 1825, in preparation for which he purchased a £90,000 silver-gilt dinner service. This is used today at Alnwick for grand dinners and pieces can still be seen in the State Dining Room (pages 86–7). He also obtained the state coach. While in Paris he bought the Paris Dagoty porcelain dessert service that is now on display in the China Gallery. Apparently, he not only paid all the expenses himself but

astonished Continental aristocrats with his generosity, semi-regal magnificence and extravagant costumes, the number of staff and their liveries, and the diamonds of his duchess.

In 1829 he was appointed Lord Lieutenant of Ireland, but not before he had suggested to the Prime Minister that the salary be reduced by one-third. The Prime Minister, the Duke of Wellington, replied, 'We are perfectly aware that the salary of office is no consideration to you . . . but it is not reasonable to expect that a nobleman should ruin himself, by undertaking to perform the duties of an office, of which the salary, together with his own means, could not defray the reasonable expense.'

In 1830, the 3rd Duchess, Charlotte Florentia, was appointed by William IV as governess to Princess Victoria, heir to the throne and later Queen Victoria. Her role was not to teach the princess maths but to be a social chaperone, in an attempt by William IV and his young queen, Adelaide, to keep at bay the influence of Victoria's mother, the meddling and money-grabbing Duchess of Kent. The King worried that if he died before Victoria was eighteen years old, the Duchess of Kent would become Regent.

Charlotte Florentia kept a diary and copied by hand each letter to the King and Queen at Windsor, and their letters to her. These were sent and returned within hours by horseriders. They tell us that when Victoria came of age, at eighteen, and twenty days before the King died, Charlotte Florentia resigned as governess. The King and Queen were upset, and each wrote her a letter. The King, who was extremely fond of Victoria, wrote of his 'anxiety for the welfare of the princess V, and heartfelt regret', yet added, 'I shall always feel grateful to you for your endeavours to overcome as far as was possible the impediments which were thrown your way.'

Shortly after Victoria's coronation, Charlotte Florentia wrote about her visit to the new Queen at Buckingham Palace in 1838. Noting that the Duchess of Kent was still 'bickering' but that the Queen 'will not give way', she wrote, 'My reception was most gratifying and agreeable to the highest degree. I see her character forming and certainly an immense increase in decision and adherence to her own opinion. She is the picture of happiness and no appearance of being loaded with a single care. I should fear she did not go deeply into any circumstance [of public affairs]. She is most exact in transcending business but I fear she reads little else, and leaves all responsibility to her ministers.'

Duchess Charlotte Florentia introduced Victoria to her future husband, Albert, at Syon House. The house is open to the public and Queen Victoria's bedroom can be seen there.

THE 4TH DUKE

Alnwick's Keep and the state rooms look more or less the way they do today because of colossal restoration carried out in the the nineteenth century by the **4th Duke**, who commissioned the architect Anthony Salvin for the external work and Luigi Canina for the interiors.

Curiously the recent Percys who made major changes to the castle, 1st Duchess, the 4th Duke and the current 12th Duke and Duchess, did not grow up expecting to inherit the castle. The 4th Duke, Algernon, was the brother of the 3rd Duke and inherited the title when the 3rd Duke died without any children in 1847.

Since he was not the eldest son, Algernon lived his life accordingly and joined the Navy at the age of twelve. Later in life, in 1852 he was to be appointed Admiral of the Fleet but he started as a midshipman in the Mediterranean, became a lieutenant in 1811, a commander in 1814, and in 1815 was

---

ABOVE The 4th Duke, here painted by Francis Grant in the 1850s, removed the fanciful Gothic schemes of his grandmother (the 1st Duchess) and in 1854 employed the architect Anthony Salvin to upgrade the castle. But he ignored Salvin's austere ideas for the interior in favour of the Italianate designs of Luigi Canina, whom he and the 4th Duchess met in Rome.
OPPOSITE Plans of the castle showing the 4th Duke's 1856 transformation of the 1st Duchess's renovations of 1760s (*RIBA Transactions* 1856–57).

acting Captain of the *Caledonia*, whereupon he retired from the Royal Navy, aged twenty-three.

While serving in the Navy, and in subsequent years, Algernon explored the world. He sailed to Cape Town to study the southern constellations at the Cape of Good Hope. He also travelled extensively in Sudan and Egypt, where he made two journeys up the Nile by boat from Cairo, in 1827 and in 1829. He travelled in great discomfort and was often in danger; he took with him Major Orlando Felix, who recorded the trip with a hundred watercolours and drawings. In 1822 Algernon went on a Grand Tour to Italy, which perhaps helped him form his later interest in architecture, interior design and art. He wrote at the time that he was impressed in Rome by the 'magnificence of the former Tyrant of the World'.

He took a long time to get married, finally doing so at the age of fifty in 1842. His choice was the daughter of Richard, 2nd Marquess of Westminster, 21-year-old Lady Eleanor Grosvenor, whom Peel described as 'homely enough looking, and very short'.

Like Duchesses Elizabeth and Charlotte, Eleanor kept a diary. Considering what she must have heard and seen, though, this makes surprisingly dull reading. If she and her husband sailed overseas, for instance, she would say the cabin was 'very comfortable' and little more. They went for winter warmth to Portugal or Italy for long periods because her husband, the Duke, suffered from rheumatism. In the Portugal section she writes, 'It is raining and the Duke is laid up. I went for a drive with Mrs Heeley' (or Mr Heeley), which she appears to have done every day. Nevertheless, her diaries show that the couple were very social. At one dinner, held at Northumberland House, the guest list includes eight dukes, six earls, ten lords and Disraeli, plus their wives.

Her letters are more interesting, especially those between her and Lord Derby, who, on behalf of Queen Victoria, beseeched her to become Mistress of the Robes. Eleanor was having none of it, writing, 'It is absolutely necessary for my health that I should persevere in declining the honour.' The Queen made Lord Derby write again, saying, 'The Queen is evidently anxious upon the subject . . . she says "tell her the duties are not at all severe, that whenever she is unwell the Duchess of Norfolk can replace her".' Lord Derby added, 'It seems to me a great pity not to undertake an office so easy and so agreeable.' Eleanor, though, thought otherwise.

When Algernon became Duke, he focused his attention on Alnwick Castle, spending the enormous sum of around £320,000 on its total renovation. This entailed destroying the delicate and exquisite Robert Adam interiors in the revived

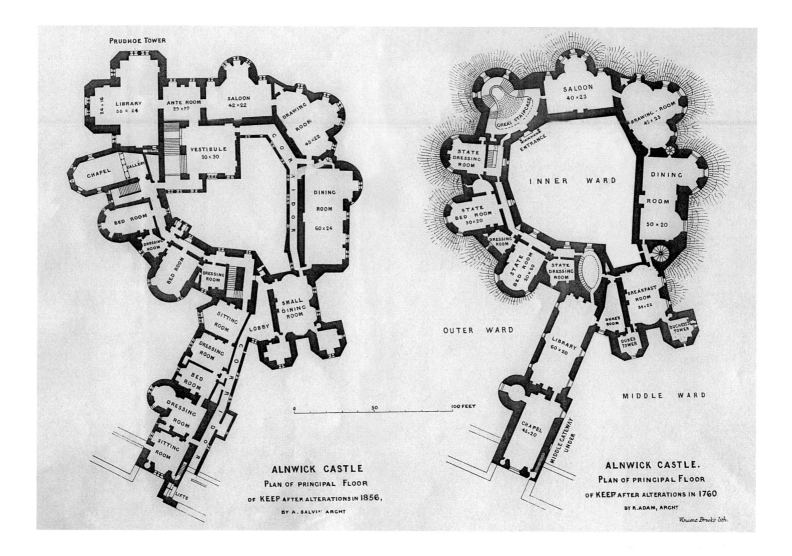

PRUDHOE TOWER

LIBRARY
56 x 24

ANTE ROOM
25 x 22

SALOON
42 x 22

DRAWING ROOM
45 x 22

VESTIBULE
30 x 30

CHAPEL

GALLERY

CORRIDOR

DINING ROOM
60 x 24

BED ROOM

DRESSING ROOM

BED ROOM

DRESSING ROOM

SITTING ROOM

LOBBY

SMALL DINING ROOM

DRESSING ROOM

BED ROOM

DRESSING ROOM

SITTING ROOM

LIFTS

0   50   100 FEET

ALNWICK CASTLE
PLAN OF PRINCIPAL FLOOR
OF KEEP AFTER ALTERATIONS IN 1856,
BY A. SALVIN ARCHT

SALOON
40 x 23

GREAT STAIRCASE

ENTRANCE

DRAWING ROOM
42 x 23

STATE DRESSING ROOM

INNER WARD

DINING ROOM
50 x 20

STATE BED ROOM
30 x 20

DRESSING ROOM

STATE BED ROOM
30 x 20

STATE DRESSING ROOM

OUTER WARD

BREAKFAST ROOM
55 x 22

DUKE'S ROOM

DUCHESS TOWER

DUKES TOWER

LIBRARY
60 x 20

MIDDLE WARD

CHAPEL
45 x 20

MIDDLE GATEWAY UNDER

ALNWICK CASTLE.
PLAN OF PRINCIPAL FLOOR
OF KEEP AFTER ALTERATIONS IN 1760
BY R. ADAM, ARCHT

Vincent Brooks lith.

Gothic style; only a hint of the stucco fantasia remains, in the hunting lodge at Hulne Priory (see page 228).

The 4th Duke employed Anthony Salvin to enhance the castle's medieval exterior and comprehensively rework and modernize the interior layout. Famous for his castle style, Salvin had also worked for the 3rd Duke at Alnwick and for Prince Albert at Windsor Castle.

If done today, the demolition of the Adam Gothic interiors would cause a national scandal. However, in an age where it was common to knock down and rebuild, that was not what was controversial about the 4th Duke's designs.

The original aim was to keep the character of a fourteenth-century border castle, but at the same time make it comfortable. Salvin drew up plans for both the exterior and the interior. However, having sent his faux-medieval Victorian-style plans in 1854, he received a reply from the Duke, who was on a long holiday in Rome with his wife. The Duke was impressed by the fact that in Italy 'seicento furnishings were to be found in medieval buildings' and told Salvin that the state rooms at Alnwick should be designed 'in the Italian style of the fifteenth and sixteenth centuries'. Ditching Salvin's plans for the interior, the Duke entrusted the interior design to

Commendatore Luigi Canina, a celebrated Italian architect and archaeologist. The only Salvin interiors at Alnwick are the old kitchens, the family 'medieval' chapel and the bones of the second and third bedroom floors.

It was Canina's Italianate interiors that caused controversy, as recorded at a meeting at the Royal Institute of British Architects (RIBA) in November 1856. Luigi Canina had died in Florence on his way back to Rome, having only just visited Alnwick and made his plans, but not before he had submitted them to RIBA for discussion. The records of the meeting also provide an explanation for the designs.

It was pointed out that the 1st Duchess's changes had caused the castle to lose 'many striking features, depriving it of its original dignity' as a medieval border fortress. Adam's layout was also considered 100 years later to be 'inconvenient', having no corridors but only room-to-room access through the castle; to the Victorians with their vast number of staff this gave no privacy. Moreover, on inheriting the castle the 4th Duke 'found a great absence of domestic comfort and a deficiency in those modern conveniences', heating and cooking being one concern. The Duke had rejected thirteenth-century internal decorations as too 'rude'

for the more 'refined . . . feelings of our time'. He had also rejected the Victorian styles of the times – in effect the work of the assembled architects – as 'variable and transitionary' and 'a creation of the passing moment'.

Understandably miffed at being forced to work with amendments by another designer, Salvin told the RIBA members, 'I had great doubts of the propriety, as well as the practicability, of introducing Italian art into a Border castle.' Others at the meeting called the Duke's plans 'infelicitious'. Nevertheless, the owner's plans went ahead regardless.

The most drastic change Salvin made at Alnwick was the demolition of two medieval towers to make way for the Prudhoe Tower, which rises well above the rest of the castle. It is so named because Algernon was known as Baron Prudhoe

ABOVE The 4th Duke and Duchess commissioned this ornate gilt-brass and ebony Napoleon III-style breakfront meuble d'appui from John Webb in 1855, for the Drawing Room. It is now on the Lovaine Corridor.

before he became Duke. Salvin's tower houses the Library and what is now the Family Kitchen below, as well as the newer family apartments above.

Salvin also moved the Chapel, attaching it to the side of the castle. The porte cochère, in the Inner Courtyard of the Keep, was added, giving cover to those arriving at the front door. Above this was made the Upper Guard Chamber, which is now a hub between the state and family rooms. Off the Upper Guard Chamber Salvin added what is now the China Gallery, a corridor that snakes around the courtyard on the first floor, alongside the Saloon, the Red Drawing Room and the State Drawing Room. This corridor is one of many clever ideas that Salvin incorporated. It allows someone to walk in an entire circle around the Keep without going through either family or state rooms, which the medieval layout did not allow.

Aside from inspiring the Italianate interior designs, the Duke and Duchess's 1853–4 trip to Paris, Frankfurt, Switzerland, Milan, Florence, Rome and Naples had a major impact on what you see today in the castle in terms of art. When in Rome they sat for Laurence Macdonald, who made busts of each of them. These are now in the Private Entrance, and someone has put a fur hat on Eleanor's head.

More significantly, it seems that, like many tourists of the time, they went to the Palazzo Cardinal Cesi to see the Baron Camuccini's famous collection of seventy-four Old Masters. Within a year the Duke had bought this entire collection and had it shipped to Liverpool dock. This collection is named after Pietro and Vincenzo Camuccini, themselves artists, who made it at the turn of the nineteenth century in Rome. The collection is of supreme examples of Italian Renaissance papal and princely patronage, such as works by Bellini, Titian, Claude, Guido Reni, Poussin, Andrea del Sarto, Badalocchio and Claude. Apart from George III's earlier purchase of fifty Canalettos from the English Consul in Venice, it is one of the greatest British acquisitions in one fell swoop by one man. Anne French, in *Art Treasures in the North: Northern Families on the Grand Tour*, says that the Camuccini purchase, 'intended to specifically complement the Italianate schemes' at Alnwick, 'at a stroke created a palace of Italian art in the North of England'.

The Duke later collected other Venetian paintings of the Renaissance, along with large monumental fresco pieces by Sebastiano del Piombo.

The Duke not only lavished money on his castle but also built new schools, churches and vicarages and rebuilt most of the farmhouses and cottages on all his estates. He also sponsored the design of self-righting lifeboats, and paid for them to be built; he donated huge sums to seamen's charities and was President of the Royal National Lifeboat Institute (as was the 2nd Duke).

The 4th Duke loved innovation and technology. He improved the agricultural estates with field drainage and created the post of His Grace's Manager of the Steam Plough. He experimented for a short time with raw sewage as fertilizer, spread by iron pipes across the fields. He was interested in the solar system and funded the publication of Herschel's observation of double stars and nebulae. In addition, as an Arabist, he initiated and funded Edward Lane's Arabic lexicon, first published in 1863.

None of the restoration or acquisitions would have occurred without a truly vast income from his estates – in particular from farm rents, coal mining and quarrying. While the Duke's wealth was for the most part inherited, its vastness was made possible by the agricultural and industrial revolutions of Queen Victoria's reign, which saw the transformation of industry and commerce by advances in finance, production and technology, as well as canal, river, road and sea developments that revolutionized transport and communication, as did the introduction of the railways from the 1840s. The Duke of Northumberland also benefited immensely from his excellent estate management. The current Duke believes that 'the 4th Duke was the highest tax- payer in the country at that time'.

While the 4th Duke and Duchess played their roles on their estate at Alnwick well with respect to traditional expectations, the couple preferred living 'in less state' at Stanwick Hall – the Yorkshire house of Algernon's grandparents, Hugh the 1st Duke and Duchess Elizabeth – and liked to spend two months each year at Kielder Castle, a modest rustic shooting lodge in vast forest lands 50 miles/80 kilometres west of Alnwick, with hardly any guests.

One wonders, therefore, what the Percys did with the incredibly grand state rooms in the castle and why the 4th Duke created them. The castle spoke for itself – there was no particular need to flaunt wealth in Northumberland. Nor was there any need to keep up with the neighbours: the Percys had long been and were still the 'uncrowned kings' of Northumberland. Perhaps the Duke's sense of his family's noble lineage and dominance dating from 1066 motivated him to create such grandeur. Perhaps it was a drive for modernity. A newspaper cutting from the time is illuminating. 'The question at issue has really been whether Alnwick Castle should be preserved as a relic and be abandoned by its owners, or whether it should undergo such a transformation.' The article also asks: should the owners 'live in a state of siege for the pleasure of antiquaries?' – a question with which today's

inhabitants would probably identify.

The Duke's exterior and interior renovations have prompted mixed responses. At one is extreme are reactions such as Sally Beauman's: she calls Alnwick's nineteenth-century state rooms 'impressive but impressive grudgingly . . . it does not work; it is gross and clumsy and oppressive and slightly mad – reminiscent of Hearst's California castle in St Simeon. Big, rich and ornate . . . It is the scale of megalomania.' Others take a different view. For instance, a newspaper article of the time, recording one of the Duke's lavish annual banquets to thank the 700 workmen at Alnwick Castle, praises the 'happy contrast' of the exterior with the interior in 'the Italian style. It may be objected that so rich an interior will not correspond with the exterior of the castle. [But] There is no incongruity between a rough casket and a brilliant gem.'

In any case, as the article also said, 'It was certainly a matter upon which [the Duke] was entitled to judge for himself.' Fortunately for him, over a hundred years ago there was nothing to stop him remodelling the castle as he wished. And while the destruction of Adam's Gothic interiors is lamentable, the practical truth is that had the 4th Duke not made these changes, no one would want to live in the castle today and it would be nothing more than a lifeless museum.

Although one of Algernon's portraits is inscribed at the bottom 'by whose taste and munificence this Castle was restored', sadly he did not live long enough to see all the work completed. When he died in 1865, his body lay in state for two days at the castle and was conveyed from Alnwick to London by special train for another lying-in-state at Northumberland House on Trafalgar Square. Admission was by ticket only for 5,000 people. Duchess Eleanor moved to Stanwick Hall and lived there until she was ninety-one years old, dying in 1911.

THE DUKES 1865–1945

The 4th Duke and his wife had no children. When he died the nearest male relative was his cousin George, who was a grandson of the 1st Duke and Duchess. George's father, Algernon Percy, 1st Earl of Beverley, was the 1st Duke and Duchess's younger son. Thus George became the **5th Duke**.

George had married Louisa Harcourt, but she died in 1848, so never became a duchess. The couple had five children. Another son is of note: Henry, who won one of the first Victoria Crosses during the Crimean War for his actions at the Battle of Inkerman in November 1854. A colonel in the Grenadier Guards, he was wounded, under heavy fire, but still relieved

General and Vice-President of the Board of Trade in 1859 in Lord Derby's second government.

After he became Duke he joined Benjamin Disraeli's second Conservative government as Lord Privy Seal in 1878, with a seat in the cabinet; he was later Lord Lieutenant of Northumberland and in 1886 was made a Knight of the Garter. He was probably one of the wealthiest members of the Cabinet: his 186,397 acres/75,432 hectares, which included the northern coal industry and ports at Tyneside, are believed to have given him an income of about £176,048 a year. Of all landowners at the time, only a few others, including the Duke of Buccleuch and the Duke of Devonshire, enjoyed an income in excess of this.

There is a great deal of evidence that the 6th Duke was extremely generous to charities, although he replied to a request by the Prime Minister's wife, Mrs Gladstone, for a contribution to the funding of a new House of Refuge to rescue prostitutes that he was 'always more inclined to assist the old and well-established Charities, which must in some degree suffer from the innumerable new ones, which spring up on all sides'.

Algernon married a banking heiress, Louisa Drummond, in 1845. Drummond's Bank exists today, run by the Royal Bank of Scotland. When Louisa's father, Henry Drummond MP, died, she and the Percy family inherited his valuable Surrey estate, including Albury House. She thus injected useful capital into the family at a time when the agricultural depression of the 1880s was affecting rents.

The 6th Duke and his wife also inherited Henry Drummond's religious ideas. The 6th Duke became involved in the late Victorian Catholic Apostolic Church in part because Henry Drummond was 'an apostle'; the seat of the Apostolic College was in fact on the Albury estate. This Christian religious sect was quite fundamentalist, placing much emphasis on ceremony, ritual and the literal truth of the Bible, and adherents prayed for the second coming of Jesus Christ as soon as possible. The couple's son and grandson, the 7th and the 8th Dukes, were much influenced by it too.

As far as the castle is concerned, Algernon and Louisa bought a lot of Victorian furniture for the private rooms, restored the Record Tower and built an underground tunnel between the kitchens and the State Dining Room in about 1890. They also reconstructed the Breakfast Room, annoyingly changing it into a dark and dreary room in the Queen Anne style; it had hitherto been the only remaining example of Robert Adam's designs and had been used by the 1st Duke and Duchess. According to the 8th Duke's 1920s book on the castle, the eighteenth-century stucco on the ceiling was 'falling to pieces'.

fifty men who were surrounded and out of ammunition, and got them back safely to camp. His sword is on display in the Lower Guard Chamber in the entrance to the castle. The current Duke's cousin, Algernon Percy, has written a good book called *A Bearskin's Crimea* about Henry's life. The 5th Duke was eighty-seven years old when he inherited the dukedom, and held it for only two years before ending up, as was the dukes' wont, in the Percy vault in Westminster Abbey.

His eldest son, Algernon, became the **6th Duke**. He was high-minded, extremely rich, a fundamentalist Christian and an active Conservative politician, and he was Duke for thirty-two years during the height of late Victorian Britain's industrialization and Empire building.

Before he became Duke in 1867, he had served as Civil Lord of the Admiralty between 1858 and 1859, and as Paymaster-

ABOVE Gustav Pope's portrait of the 5th Duke, 1866, hanging in the State Dining Room. When Algernon, the 4th Duke, died he and his wife had no children. The next male relative was George, who came from the Beverley line and was a grandson of the 1st Duke and Duchess. Duke George was eighty-seven years old when he inherited the title and died two years later.

Around this time William Armstrong, later made a baron, was building Cragside near by at Rothbury in what is called the Free Tudor style. Indeed the Duke sold some of his land to Armstrong for the house. Armstrong was a Tyneside industrialist, hydraulic innovator and engineer. Accordingly, his new house was the first in the world to be lit entirely by hydro-electricity. He was also one of the first people to consider renewable energy, saying coal 'was used wastefully and extravagantly in all its applications'. As the Duke was one of the coal barons of Britain, perhaps Armstrong and the Duke were not destined to like each other. When in 1884 the Prince and Princess of Wales came to Northumberland on an official visit, they chose to stay with Armstrong rather than at Alnwick, which cannot have helped matters. Not to be outdone, the Duke installed hydro-electricity at Alnwick Castle in 1889. It powered the lights for the state rooms until after the Second World War. The current Duke has recently restored this Victorian hydro-powered contraption and it now supplies the sawmills.

In 1874 Northumberland House, the Percy family's London residence since the seventeenth century and a prime example of English Renaissance architecture, was in the way of plans to connect Trafalgar Square with the new road along the Embankment (Northumberland Avenue) and Parliament wanted it demolished. Understandably, the Duke was reluctant to leave, but really had no choice in the matter, and this fine house was pulled down. He received £500,000 in compensation. The 1st Duchess's Robert Adam Glass Drawing Room from the house remains, in part, at the Victoria & Albert Museum in London. The upside to this architectural slaughter is that some of the Northumberland House furniture and chandeliers were moved up to the castle, giving Alnwick today a sense of fullness. Thomas Williams, the steward at the time, wrote a very detailed account of Northumberland House before it was demolished – he went through the house, room by room, and described everything – and there are some photographs of it in the archives.

The 6th Duke and Duchess had two sons, of whom the elder, Henry, became the **7th Duke** when his father died in 1899. Henry inherited the title in his mid-fifties, and was Duke for just under twenty years until he died six months before the end of the First World War.

He married Edith Douglas Campbell, the eldest daughter of George Douglas, 8th Duke of Argyll. Edith was the first Duchess of Northumberland to come from Scotland. In fact all the Dukes since have married Scots. Duchess Edith founded and ran a county nursing association. As was common with the late Victorians, she and Henry had a large family of thirteen children. Although Henry became Duke at the turn of the twentieth century, he was not comfortable with modernity and dressed like a mid-Victorian aristocrat.

Like many of his predecessors, the 7th Duke was an MP, Lord Lieutenant, Lord Treasurer of the Royal Household, and the elected Chairman of Northumberland County Council for twenty-three successive years. 'He was not a man who dazzled the world, and aspired to anything but dazzling it,' reads one obituary. Reading between the lines of other hat-doffing eulogies, one understands that he was a man who fulfilled his duties in a conscientious manner. His younger son writes of his father that he was inherently wary of the 'infection of idleness that haunts a leisured society' and 'his very vivid moral sense was one of personal duty to a personal neighbour' and reflects: 'my chief impression of my parents is of an immensely laborious life'. He was a philanthropist and contributed generously to many good causes, including housing associations and the building of schools such as the Duke's School in Alnwick, which cost £15,000.

In 1906 the 7th Duke and his wife hosted a royal visit to Alnwick Castle by Edward VII and Queen Alexandra. The castle archives reveal the extraordinary effort put into the visit, especially as to the vast number of horses and carriages and who sat where. In return for their hospitality, the 7th Duke and Duchess were presented with bronze busts of the King and Queen, now in the China Gallery. After the visit, the King's private secretary wrote to the Duke, 'I have told the King in accordance with your wish, that you very much appreciated his Bust. Believe me.'

Two years later, the Prince and Princess of Wales came to stay for a week, from 29 June to 6 July 1908. During their visit, the royal couple went by train to the Royal Agricultural Show in Newcastle. The Duchess organized luncheon on the Royal Train of *salade de saumon*, *poulet froid* and *cotelettes d'agneau chaudes*, *asperges* with *sauce mousseline* – to start with. The main course was *boeuf pressé*, *jambon*, tongue and *salade de saison*. The savoury was omelette Clairemonte, followed by *glacé*, and then 'dessert, and café'.

The archives show that the household bill for food during the royal visit was £99 for fruit and vegetables; £16 for turtle soup; £51 for the butcher; £40 for bacon, tongue and hams; and £208 for fish, fowl and turkey. Some of the dinners at the castle that week were for forty people. Other payments relating to the royal visit came to £1,828, including three Prince of Wales standards costing £14.

The Duke wrote to his household afterwards to thank

them, saying, 'It must have entailed a great deal of work, and arrangement, and having to keep it up for a whole week must have been very tiring for everybody but it was all satisfactorily managed . . . and passed off without a hitch of any kind.' The Duke was later rewarded by being made Lord High Steward at George V's coronation in 1911, at which he bore St Edward's Crown.

Alan Ian Percy was not the eldest son of the 7th Duke, but he was the eldest surviving fourth son and therefore became the **8th Duke** on his father's death in 1918. Curiously, the 1st, 4th and 10th Dukes were all second sons, as is the current 12th Duke. Although he was Duke throughout the 1920s, which have a reputation for frivolity, he was in character an Edwardian and Imperialist. He was deeply concerned about current affairs, which included, only two months after his father's death, the execution of Tsar Nicholas II and its consequences.

The 8th Duke was a staunch Conservative, very involved with politics and, like his grandfather, influenced by the teachings of the fundamentalist Catholic Apostolic Church. He partly funded *The Post*, which later merged into the *Daily Telegraph*. He also founded a journal called *The Patriot*, a leading right-wing weekly inter-war newspaper. Among other things, he was opposed to the League of Nations and to Communism.

Before he became Duke, he was a keen huntsman and had a long military background, serving in the Boer War in South Africa and then in Sudan. In 1910 he was made ADC to the Governor-General of Canada.

Becoming Duke as the First World War was ending, he had to manage the effects of the aftermath of the war on the Percy estates. When the 7th Duke died in 1918 he left an estate valued at £1,108,000. By this time, the top rate of inheritance tax had doubled from 20 per cent, before 1914, to 40 per cent, and the Chancellor of the Exchequer, Lloyd George, had introduced a supertax on the incomes of the rich. The post-war economy and death duties meant that in order for the main Percy estates to survive, certain properties needed to be sold. Consequently, in 1922 the 8th Duke sold the house and estate of Stanwick Park and Kielder Castle. The house had served as a military hospital during the First World War. Permanent custodianship of Warkworth Castle was given to the forerunners of English Heritage. Nothing of any consequence was done structurally to Alnwick Castle during the 8th Duke's reign.

His great blessing was his marriage to Lady Helen Magdalen Gordon-Lennox, daughter of the Duke of Richmond. Alan and Helen had six children. Between them, the Duke and Duchess continued their traditional role of leadership in the county. It is a leadership that is hard to define, though it is equally hard to deny it existed.

The Duchess was called by newspapers of the time 'our democratic Duchess', which seems a contradiction in terms. But what is clear from the archives is that she was extremely accomplished, considered the epitome of charm and highly respected. She was a traditionalist who never forgot the heritage of her family and the service it implied. She regularly appeared at the Duchess's School in Alnwick for prize-givings. After she was widowed in 1930, she helped to bring the family and its interests through the Second World War intact, particularly after the death of her eldest son in Flanders in 1940.

It is said that as a girl she was an outstanding beauty, with spun-gold hair. Philip de László painted her three times, in 1917, in the late 1920s and again in 1937 when she was Mistress of the Robes to Queen Elizabeth (later the Queen Mother) after the coronation of George VI. She was a close friend of both Queen Mary and Queen Elizabeth and remained Mistress of the Robes until 1964.

One of her first duties was to immediately follow the Queen in procession at the coronation of her husband, George VI, in 1937. After the shock of Edward VIII's abdication, society approved of the Queen's new 'nice woman' at court. Queen Victoria Eugenia of Spain's lady-in-waiting wrote, 'The Duchess of Northumberland is a saint, the sort of woman who rides in buses, pays her bills, and is nice to old servants.' Quite an understated yet charming description of the daughter of a duke who married a duke, and whose majestic bearing and huge diamonds impressed many at the coronation.

Cecil Beaton later mentions her in his diaries when he describes Elizabeth II's first state opening of Parliament in November 1952: 'The Mistress of the Robes, the Duchess of Northumberland, gigantically tall with wonderful jewels, wore a Knightsbridge horror of a dress, a crinoline of coarse, Parma violet nylon-tulle with self-same sausages, that was so daring in its bad taste that the effect was wonderful.'

In 1930, Duchess Helen made important inventories of the collections at Alnwick, Syon and Albury, which are like a personally annotated photo-guidebook. As we know, the 8th Duke, too, wrote a guidebook of the castle.

When her second son (by then the 10th Duke) married in 1946, she handed over the whole of her public life in Northumberland to his bride. She, now the Dowager Duchess Elizabeth, recalls, 'She was quite a strict lady. She looked very grand – was quite tall and stately. However, an absolutely sweet person. I was nervous

Cecil Beaton / *Vogue* © The Condé Nast Publications Ltd.

of her to begin with because she looked so overpowering, but she was kind and gentle and we got on really well.'

The current Duke, her grandson, remembers her in his childhood. 'She was a really kind lady. We slightly took advantage of her when she became a little bit gaga, as at Christmas she would stand at the top of the table and hand out pound notes to her grandchildren, so we worked out if we went round the table twice we could get another one or two.'

When the future Edward VIII visited Alnwick as Prince of Wales in July 1923 the reception on his arrival was a great event for the castle and the town and involved many people, including bands and soldiers. The Prince caused a ducal flutter beforehand. On hearing only six days before his planned arrival that 'we are still unsure of the Prince's movements, there appears to be a idea he comes on a later train,' the 8th Duke replied curtly: 'It is now very late to think of altering the whole plan, and I hope they will adhere to the original proposal. The majority of my guests are coming on it [the train] and it will complicate everything if changes are made.'

The Prince showed more sympathy for the costs. With the economy being depressed at the time, he 'expressed the wish

OPPOSITE In this photograph taken in July 1906, Queen Alexandra sits in the centre, wearing a dark dress. On the left is Edith, 7th Duchess of Northumberland; to the right is Edward VII, the Countess of Pembroke and the Duke of Northumberland. On the far left sits Earl Percy, the heir, who was to die three years later of 'acute pleurisy' in a Paris hotel aged thirty-six. His younger brother Alan became the 8th Duke in 1918.

ABOVE This portrait of the current Duke's grandmother Helen, the 8th Duchess, called 'Heds' by her family, by Cecil Beaton was published in *Vogue*'s September edition in 1937, the year of George VI's coronation.

that, in time of distress like the present, no expenditure be incurred by the Public Authorities and that any display of bunting should be left to individual house owners'. Great lists for the royal welcome were drawn up, detailing who got admission tickets to the Castle Square or the Barbican, including 240 employees, 750 tenants and 1,400 schoolchildren.

Duchess Helen asked the housekeeper to get 'three fresh run salmon'; the Duke's piper was telegrammed with instructions; passes for photographers were drawn up; eighteen guests were invited to join the house party; and the seven-car motorcade from the station to the castle was all planned to the last detail, including a stop at the church, requested by the vicar, so that the children could see the Prince. The Prince set off from London's King's Cross at 10.00 a.m. and arrived at Alnwick seven hours later at 5.17 p.m. precisely. Today the same train journey takes three and a half hours.

Long programmes were made for each day's royal activities, one being a visit to the Royal Agricultural Show in Newcastle in a motorcade of eleven cars. This included a ten-minute address by the Prince at important towns en route to Newcastle. The royal party returned to the castle at 9.15 p.m. for dinner. Other houseguests included the Duke and Duchess of Richmond and Gordon, the Duke and Duchess of Portland and the Duchess of Sutherland.

Duke Alan died in 1930, leaving an estate estimated at £2,510,000. Duchess Helen died in 1965, aged seventy-eight.

Their eldest son, Henry, was eighteen years old when he became **9th Duke**. On his coming of age in 1933, the tenantry

gave him the only painting made of him as an adult in his lifetime, showing him seated on his favourite horse, Brown Bird – he was fond of hunting – and his mother sent him off to travel the world. During this time he went to Africa, and many of the exotic animal heads and skins currently at Hulne Priory, or in the Duchess's kitchen, date from these trips.

At the start of the Second World War in 1939 Henry was a lieutenant in the Grenadier Guards. In late 1939 he went with the regiment's three regular battalions to Belgium and France as part of the British Expeditionary Force. German units pushed through the Ardennes to cut off and surround the Allied units that had advanced into Belgium. In the face of the *blitzkrieg*, or lightning war, strategy that German units deployed against British forces, the Grenadier Guards battalions fought to maintain the British Army's position before being evacuated from Dunkirk along with 338,000 or so other men between 26 May and 3 June 1940. Henry, the 9th Duke, was not among them. He had been killed by German forces at Pecq in Flanders, Belgium, on 21 May 1940. He was twenty-seven, and so was both the youngest Percy to become Duke and the youngest Duke to die. Mr Hugonin, the Northumberland Estates agent from 1962, says, 'I have heard it said that he took a rather fatalistic view. I mean, he knew he was going to be killed.'

Henry is the last member of the Percy family to have died in conflict, the first being William de Percy, who was killed on a crusade. Algernon Percy dedicates his book *A Bearskin's Crimea* to the 9th Duke, and says that his heroic final actions echoed

those of his ancestor Henry Percy, VC, in the Crimean War.

Although Henry was considered the most eligible bachelor in the country, he died unmarried and was therefore succeeded by his brother Hugh. There is a posthumous portrait of him in the Upper Guard Chamber by Oswald Birley in 1947.

Newspaper reports of his death focused on the crippling demands of heavy death duties his estate would face, noting that only twelve years earlier, in 1930, the 'Treasury claimed not less than £1,255,000 (50 per cent) of the family fortune.' Under the Death Duties Act of 1914 no duties were charged on the estates of soldiers who died in action, but this was meant to be applied to only the first £5,000 of an estate.

The newspapers also reported that the young Duke and his mother had 'struggled hard to keep open the Castle . . . but just over a year ago [1939] they had to give up the fight. Taxation beat them and they closed the Castle.'

OPPOSITE Edward, Prince of Wales, visiting in 1923, sitting between the Alan, 8th Duke, and his wife Helen. The flippant Prince annoyed the conservative Duke with last-minute dithering over his arrival in Alnwick.

ABOVE Widowed in 1930, Helen, 8th Duchess (left), helped to bring the family through the Second World War, particularly after the death of her eldest son, Henry, 9th Duke (right), in Flanders in 1940. She died in 1965 at the age of seventy-eight. Henry died aged twenty-seven fighting Nazi forces before the Battle of Dunkirk.

ALNWICK CASTLE AFTER THE WAR

Before the Second World War, and like his elder brother, the **10th Duke** was schooled at Eton, where he hunted the college's beagles, although a bad knee smash made him give up that pursuit. From Eton, he went to Oxford, and was studying for the Parliamentary Bar when the Second World War broke out. By the time he was thrust into the position of Duke by the death of his brother in 1940, he, his mother and siblings had moved out of the castle to Lesbury House, 4 miles/6.5 kilometres away, where his mother lived until she died. During the war, evacuated schoolgirls from the Church High School, Jesmond, Newcastle, used the castle as a boarding school.

Keeping up the tradition of 'the fighting Percys', the young Duke served in the Northumberland Hussars until 1944. He fought with his regiment and Allied troops to defend Greece from the onslaught of the German Twelfth Army invasion in April 1941. Greek and British Commonwealth forces fought with great bravery, but were vastly outnumbered and outgunned by another overwhelming Nazi attack by land and air, and by May 1941 Greece was occupied by the Nazis. The Duke also took part in the defence of Crete, but again the Nazis were victorious. Fortunately he survived, ended up in Cairo and was able to cable his mother, Duchess Helen, in July 1941 that he was 'safe and well'.

During the war Hugh – known by friends as Hughie – determined to marry Lady Elizabeth Montagu Douglas Scott, daughter of the Duke and Duchess of Buccleuch and Queensberry, which he did in 1946. During the war she served first in a canteen, then in a military hospital and from 1942 as a Wren officer. Her war experience contrasted sharply with her husband's, as she explains: 'I had a wonderful war, if anybody can have a wonderful war. I had a trip out to Australia by sea to New York, train to San Francisco. Then a plane called the *Martin Mars*, the biggest flying boat ever built, flew us and about twelve Wrens and a few sailors out to Australia via different islands across the Pacific. Which was fascinating.

'We arrived in Australia January '45 when the war was spreading out to the Pacific. All our forces were up in the Islands, with the Americans. I was a coder, a signal officer. It was frightfully complicated – a question of adding and subtracting figures from one another to get the code. I happened to be on duty the night when VE-Day was announced. At five o'clock in the morning came a signal that I decoded with great excitement saying that peace had been declared in Europe. I

had to go round saying "The war is over," which of course it wasn't because the war in the Pacific was still going on.'

Duchess Elizabeth (as the Dowager Duchess is known) describes how she first met her husband. 'He used to come and hunt with us when I was a little girl. He always liked friends of older people really. So he was great friends with my parents. He didn't take much notice of me to begin with. Except I had this little pony, so he rather admired the way I went. They all went off to the hunt ball without me and he said he wished I was coming to the hunt ball too but I was too young. That pleased me anyway and I remembered it.'

She remembers seeing the castle during the war: 'He was very cross with me for going to Australia – he said I needn't have gone. I said, "But the war is going on so I must go. My orders." When I came back at the beginning of 1946 on the *Aquitania* I did say I must see my friends first, which annoyed him. Then I went to stay at Lesbury House, as a guest of his mother. Petrol was rationed but he had an old car and they took me up to the castle to look at it. All the furniture in the castle was piled in the big dining room, so the rest of the castle was empty and looked like a shell. It didn't look very cosy. I was a bit, I suppose, horrified at the idea of living in this vast place.'

Notwithstanding the fact that Elizabeth was Scottish and also a Douglas (the Douglases were ancient enemies of the Percys) she and Hugh were married in 1946, the first society couple to be married at Westminster Abbey following the end of the Second World War. The wedding was a huge occasion, watched by vast crowds. Guests included Queen Mary, Queen Elizabeth and George VI along with Princess Elizabeth (the

future Queen Elizabeth II), and her sister, Princess Margaret, as well as the Duchess of Gloucester, the bride's aunt.

The newly married couple moved into the castle almost immediately. 'But first we went to Albury for our honeymoon. Then we went up to Inverness-shire, where my mother-in-law had a house – that was their annual routine. I got to know her quite well then, washed her hair for her and learned to fish. One had to throw oneself into what the Percys liked doing. Every Percy fished all their lives. I never had, but I have now.

'We moved into the castle at Christmas in 1946 when there was deep snow everywhere. It was bitterly cold with three foot of snow all around it. My new miniature poodle had fluffy curls, so every time he came in I had to sit on the doorstep taking the snow off his curls. Of course, when I first lived up here, I knew nobody in this area and my husband had various very old friends like the vicar and his wife – or the Brigadier and his wife, who bored one to bits. My husband used to like taking the husband off to the sitting room after dinner for a drink and I would be left with the boring wife for hours. That was for the first three months and we moved to Syon for the summer. I had never been to Syon before.'

Once back at the castle, Duchess Elizabeth moved the furniture back into place and over time began to settle in. 'The castle really became very cosy. I felt it was homely despite it being, you know, what it is. I felt very happy there. I had a bedroom at the far end of the Warkworth Corridor. My late husband's dressing room was the far end of the Warkworth Corridor, and mine was the next lovely room. It looked right over the river towards the sea. The boudoir [now the Private Dining Room] was my sitting-room-cum-drawing-room-cum-everything. We didn't use the Library for quite a long time. I suppose when the children needed more space we did.'

The couple had seven children: Lady Caroline, Lady Victoria, Lady Julia, Henry (the 11th Duke), Ralph (the 12th Duke), and the youngest, Lord James. A seventh child died when a baby.

In the years of austerity following the Second World War, and because of the supertax on high income and death duties, few changes were made to the interior of the castle. 'Oh no, I wasn't allowed to do any changes – nothing like that – no,' Duchess Elizabeth says. 'Except the Library carpet. I remember having great arguments because it was threadbare and I think I eventually took a crashing fall on it. So my husband allowed me to get a new carpet for the Library but up until then it was no change. I mean there was no money, for one thing.' She was also allowed to lay a new carpet in the corridor outside her boudoir for a royal visit in 1982.

Ian August, who started work as the estate's Clerk of Works

in 1955 and served the 10th Duke, recalls that the Duke 'wanted to have a vanity basin put into his bedroom so that he could shave. And I said, looking at the peeling walls, "Well, while we are doing this, Your Grace, do you think we should maybe think of redecorating?" And he said, '"Well, how old is this wallpaper, August?" I said, "It was put on earlier this century, Your Grace." "Is that all?" the Duke replied.'

One of Duke Hugh's innovations was opening the castle for the first time ever to the public in 1950. The move was driven by economic necessity rather than a desire to greet

OPPOSITE The current Duke's mother, then Lady Elizabeth Montagu Douglas Scott, served as a cypher officer in the Women's Royal Naval Service, in troop ships on the Atlantic run during the height of the U-boat campaign and later in the Pacific. 'My last few days of sunshine in Australia' is her caption to this photograph (right), taken before she left for England in December 1945.

ABOVE Lady Elizabeth, aged twenty-four, married the 10th Duke at Westminster Abbey on 12 June 1946. The wedding was attended by George VI, Queen Elizabeth, Princess Elizabeth, Princess Margaret, Queen Mary and Princess Marina, Duchess of Kent, and Princess Alice, Duchess of Gloucester, the Duchess's aunt. The bride wore a white satin dress, the Buccleuch diamond and pearl tiara, and the Northumberland pearls, a gift from the Duke. After a reception at Admiralty House, the newly married couple, pictured (right) in their going-away outfits, spent part of their honeymoon in Killarney, Ireland.

thousands of strangers. On opening the castle, the Duke said to his agent, Mr Hugonin, 'I am not going to spend money trying to get people to come to Alnwick Castle. If they want to come and see my home and where I live, well, I'll say, let them come, but I am not going to make it all right for them – I want it right for myself.'

Mr Hugonin explains the estate's early approach to tourism. 'Heritage became a word during his last years. He derived a certain amount of amusement that he was part of the heritage. That didn't mean that he wasn't aware of the family history. But he never really wanted to face up to the longer-term cost of keeping the castle going as a building.'

If little was done inside aside from 'patch and mend', outside was different. Hugh brought the estate through the difficult post-war years until productivity improved in the 1980s and rent restrictions were lifted after 1979. Nevertheless his style was 'old school'. 'He hated discussion of money or the accounts. "Never fall down and worship at the feet of the god of economics," I can remember him saying to me once,' says Mr Hugonin. 'If we found that the estate was in the red he would say, "Well, I will have to sell something." He did so a lot – but minor pieces of the collection, nothing major.'

The nationalization of the coal industry in 1946 deprived the estate of its coal revenue and it subsequently survived on rents for many decades. But housing and agricultural rents were low, restricted by laws such as the Agricultural Holdings Acts of 1947 and 1948. In any case, the Duke was averse to rent rises. 'Remember,' the Duke warned his agent, 'after you have been I still expect to be able to have a drink in any farmhouse on the estate!' The point for him was 'to keep a hunt going, to have a good shoot and to make sure that the tenants were happy'.

The Percys are an outdoor family and no one more so than this Duke. 'He really thought that hunting was more important than anything else. The Percy foxhounds were a major department of the estate and reported directly to the Duke,' explains Mr Hugonin. Hunting was not just about pleasure, though. Ian August remembers: 'When he came back in the afternoon from the hunt he would come back into the office and see his secretary. He had the ability to absorb all this information gathered throughout the day that related to work on the estate. He would be hunting three days a week over his own land with his tenants. And so there was this personal contact. If they did not hunt, he was passing over the land and would meet up with them anyway. So while he was enjoying himself through the hunt he was actually doing business.'

As might be expected, the Duke and Duchess were both actively involved in public life. The 10th Duke held many posts, including royal ones, namely Lord Lieutenant of Northumberland and Lord Steward of Her Majesty's Household. The Duchess recalls: 'Somebody called up, saying is my husband home, and I said no he wasn't and then they said that they had made him Lord Steward. I said, "Oh no, have you? Oh, he won't like that sort of thing," before I could stop myself. He hated anything to do with pomp and ceremony.'

The 10th Duke took part in the coronation of Elizabeth II in 1953. The Duchess says of the occasion, 'I was about to have Harry. He was born two weeks later. So I asked if I could have an interview with the Duke of Norfolk to see if, supposing things went wrong and I had to leave the Abbey, it would be possible. And he was absolutely sweet about it and said don't worry just put your hand up and one of my chaps will come and take you to hospital.'

Duke Hugh served as chairman of committees relating to either agriculture or education, such as the Agriculture Research Council, the Committee of Enquiry on Foot and Mouth Disease and the Medical Research Council. He was also Chancellor of Newcastle University. Indeed, education was one of his passions. He thought that the many empty Victorian staff quarters attached to the Outer Bailey should be used. At first he leased them to Northumberland County Council for use as a teacher training college and from 1981 he rented them to St Cloud State University, Minnesota.

In Duchess Elizabeth's albums, there are masses of photographs and newspaper cuttings showing her at endless functions, smiling and confident. Yet after decades of public service she reveals the inner struggle it entailed. 'I just had to get on with it. I mean, one of the very first things was they asked me to be Chairman of the Governors of the Duchess School. I have never been to school in my life. I always had to make a prize-giving speech. So, one's whole life was rather wrecked by doing those things, which didn't come naturally to me at all. That was always an effort.' It seems, though, that her confidence grew. 'I remember sitting at one of these state banquets, next to one of those very socialist ministers and being inquisitioned about one's life and being able to retort that I was a rating in the navy so I know all about the other side of life. That settled things.'

It is said that in private the Duke and Duchess were great fun. The Duke was a good mimic and had, according to Mr Hugonin, 'an enormous sense of humour but dry and self-deprecating'. Apparently he was once on a shooting lunch with another duke, who was not considered a popular figure and was bemoaning the fact that it was difficult for dukes to have and make friends. To which Duke Hugh said, out of earshot, 'My dear Bo Bo, if you weren't a Duke you wouldn't have any friends.'

They entertained frequently, their guests including Queen Elizabeth the Queen Mother, and Queen Elizabeth and Prince Philip, who came to stay at the castle in May 1982, when the Queen opened the giant Kielder Dam. Apparently, the Queen greatly enjoyed her visit and she told Duchess Elizabeth that it was wonderful to see the beautiful views of the English countryside on their drive around Hulne Park, which she found restorative in the midst of the worry of the Falklands War. The Queen's son, Prince Andrew, was serving in the war at the time, and a secret telephone line had to be installed in Alnwick Castle so that the Queen could keep up with military developments during her stay. Staff said they were in awe of her huge burgundy Rolls Royce which, parked in the stable yard, was often being polished by her drivers.

When the 10th Duke's eldest son Henry – or Harry, as he preferred to be known – was born in 1953, the beacon-like fire at the top of Brizlee Tower in the park was lit, as always happens when the first son of a Duke of Northumberland is born, and the Queen agreed to be a godmother. Harry went on to be educated at Eton, and Christ Church, Oxford. He became **11th Duke** on his father's death in 1988.

As the 11th Duke, Harry tended to live at Syon more

to protect African wildlife, including African elephants, and is now supported by Prince William, the Duke of Cambridge.

Ian August remembers Harry. 'I felt he was always uncomfortable up here because he was more at home at Syon in the London scene where he could just melt into what was happening. At the castle he was this prominent figure whom everybody looked at. They were all waiting to shoot him down and find fault with what he was doing. I had a lot of time for him because I had known him since he was young child.' Once he became Duke, we looked after him. I would come across at five o'clock at night, there would be a pot of tea or coffee and a big box of biscuits, and we would sit in the dining room. He liked talking about filming or how we could restore various things in the castle but the trouble was he never really got round to doing any of it.'

One of the difficulties, of course, was that money was not available. 'When Harry took over there wasn't a very positive attitude in the economy outside the walls of the castle and that was reflected in what was happening inside – we were really just treading water,' says Ian August.

Harry's mother, Duchess Elizabeth, candidly reveals: 'My poor son Harry when he inherited, you know, he suffered from a sort of depression. I always had to boost him up.'

The estate languished during this period, Ian August recalls. 'There was a change of strategy because after working for a duke who for thirty years had led this estate, the agent, Bill Hugonin, had to take on a major role above what he was before because of the fact that he wasn't getting the same sort of direction from the new Duke.' During Harry's time as Duke his younger brother Ralph took the chair at important estate meetings – 'very reluctantly', adds Ian.

The future for the castle looked bleak. 'You could see a situation where this building might not be retained as a family home,' Ian August recalls. 'I could see that in Harry's time it could have got to a point where this just became a museum – showing people how people had lived in the past.'

Harry died overnight of an accidental overdose in 1995, in the same bedroom at Syon House as the one his father died in. His butler, Brinley, found Harry dead on the floor in the morning with the telephone in his hands. It is believed that the young Duke, who was on antidepressants, got muddled about the correct dose and took too many late in the night.

than Alnwick. He was a keen film fan, setting up his own production company, called Hotspur Films. The actor Sir Timothy Ackroyd first met Harry at the Apollo Theatre and in an article remembers a 'gentle man possessed of a quiet charm with whom I felt immediately at ease'. He says that Harry's film *Lost in Africa* remains as 'a great achievement.' It was filmed in tough, hot and uncomfortable locations and he remembers sitting under a canopy, rain pouring outside, as Harry handed out his 'ever present menthol cigarettes' to delighted and gleeful Samburu warriors. Sir Timothy especially valued Harry's contribution as a trustee and patron of the conservation charity Tusk, which was founded to help

---

ABOVE LEFT The 10th Duchess at the wedding ball at Windsor Castle given by the Queen and Prince Philip for Princess Alexandra and Mr Angus Ogilvy in 1963. It was the first time for ages that German princes and archdukes had attended a British royal wedding. The ball was meant to end at two a.m. but the Queen danced until three.
ABOVE RIGHT In June 1962 the Queen Mother came to stay at the castle. Landing at Newcastle Airport in a red Heron aircraft of the Queen's Flight, she was met by Hugh, 10th Duke, before they went on to Gosforth Park to see her horse Harvest Gold run in the Durham Plate.

THE 12TH DUKE AND DUCHESS

Harry, the 11th Duke, was forty-two when he died, and while he had had numerous girlfriends, he had never married, so the dukedom passed to his brother, Lord Ralph Percy, who became the **12th Duke** and his wife, Lady Percy, the Duchess.

'The sad and premature death of my brother Harry has thrown my family and myself into a position that some may envy but others will sympathize with,' said the 12th Duke to the estate soon after he inherited in 1995. It was clearly not a situation he had anticipated, as he recently explained to me. 'I was born in 1956 and I am the fifth out of seven children, and so it is a bit strange to be back living here now, and being in charge of this place.' But whatever the personal rewards or the disadvantages associated with the position and the more public image that came with it, as well as the responsibilities, the Duke's succession marked a renaissance for the castle.

'My father always thought that one day he would have to build a house somewhere out in the park and he wouldn't be able to maintain the castle,' says the Duke. 'There was a definite feeling throughout my childhood that we were living in a golden age and it probably wouldn't go on.' That the Percy family still live in Alnwick today is due to this Duke and Duchess.

They married in 1979. The Duchess is the daughter of John Walter Maxwell Miller Richard, former chairman of the Scottish Stock Exchange and once owner of a fort at Charge Law Plantation. Her mother is Angela, Lady Buchan Hepburn, who owns an important garden at Kailzie, in the Scottish borders in Peeblesshire. The Duke and Duchess have four children: Lady Catherine Valentine, born in 1982; George, born in 1984 and known as Earl Percy; Lady Melissa Percy, born in 1987; and Lord Max Percy, born in 1990.

Energetic, modern and informal in style, the Duchess dislikes anything 'twin set, pearls and duchessey', and refuses to be photographed in a tiara. Being a duchess, she says, is simply a job. On the other hand, she continues with the Percy tradition of good works by being patron, president or vice president of eighty charities relating to a wide range of issues, especially those relating to horticulture, children and the elderly; she is also interested in medicine, including issues relating to special needs, mental health and cancer. In 2009, she was made Lord Lieutenant of Northumberland, which the Dowager Duchess Elizabeth thinks was a good idea. 'It saves Ralph, who is much shier, you know.' Yet there can be nothing more traditional than slaving to restore one's husband's heritage for future generations, as she has done.

If it felt strange for the Duke moving back into the castle where he grew up, it was equally a revelation for the new Duchess, who felt she was moving into 'an old museum'. Keen to make a family home, she embarked on the most major restoration since that of Algernon, the 4th Duke, in the 1850s. This included structural restorations of the castle's outer walls. The lead roof was replaced. The private side was entirely redesigned. In addition, the State Dining Room was restored completely in 2006, then the Saloon and in 2009 the Drawing Room. At the same time, the Duchess restored and rebuilt the garden – a story in its own right, and pictured on pages 203–25.

Inside the castle, it is clear that the Duchess has a great eye for detail and for creating a pleasing atmosphere. Though she is not intellectually interested in the history of decorative arts *per se*, she is extremely interested in conserving the state rooms to the highest standards possible. 'My taste is for the comfortable and welcoming without pinpointing a date. I love beautiful woods with wonderful grains, like burr elm or limed oak. But I tend not to like dark furniture of any description.' Fortunately, since she has inherited a lot of it, she likes Georgian and French Louis furniture. 'But it has to be in the right context,' she adds. 'No matter how much I liked French provincial, for example, I might put it in another house or in a bedroom here but you obviously couldn't use it in the state rooms,' she explains. 'The only style I really don't like is Art Deco.'

The Duchess has also overseen the restoration of the art collection. However, 'If money were no object, I'd love to collect contemporary art, adding to the collection with the best of the twenty-first century,' she reveals.

Her taxidermy collection, on display in many of the castle's rooms, reveals another side to the Duchess. Indeed, she has a perverse interest in death and ghoulish things like poison; as well as making a Poison Garden at Alnwick she has written novels on the subject of poison. These tales of gothic love, revenge and the dangerous world of poisonous plants were inspired by her Poison Garden in the Alnwick Garden. 'I looked at datura plants growing next to strychnine and hemlock in the Poison Garden. I imagined what incredible stories they could tell. So, this is how my idea for *The Poison Diaries* came about.'

One of the things she is most proud of is the gate to the new family graveyard. On her death, she wants some of her ashes to be put into hourglass egg timers, so that her children can remember her each breakfast time. Planning ahead, she

asked a grand London jeweller for a quotation for making these, which caused some confusion when it was mistakenly sent to her mother-in-law, Duchess Elizabeth.

The size of the castle makes it an unusual home, and the Duchess admits, 'I haven't been in some parts of it. I wouldn't know how to find my way around some of the wings – say, where the American students are. But although it is big it actually feels very cosy and homely – it has got a really good atmosphere and there is nothing spooky about it.' Asked if the family call it home, the house or the castle, she replies, 'It is half and half. We say we're going home but we also call it the house, and sometimes it is called the castle – so a bit of everything. Basically it is home for the times that we are living here.'

A drawback of living in a castle is that 'You can feel that you are in your own little village with a wall around it. You cannot

just step outside through French doors. Nor is there a garden outside the front door, so it would be difficult to live here in the summer. Moreover, due to the design of this medieval keep, you would have to pass the summer visitors to reach it. With hundreds of thousands coming through the site that might be difficult.'

The Duchess insists that the essence of restoring the castle into a place you would want to come and live in was choosing the right team to help. Certainly in her work she confers with the finest brains, though part of her skill is in being confident to follow her own path when need be; indeed, there is something of a CEO about her.

But the castle's restoration was fundamentally possible because of the Duke's skill in turning around the fortunes of Northumberland Estates. This he did with quiet gusto, helped by not having to waste time in a quagmire of committees. 'The whole point about most of the great things done in this country is they were done by individuals. It is very important to keep that going. I do see that organizations like the National Trust have to be run by committees but here I would rather do it in an autocratic way, personally.' Today the company is focused on conservation, heritage, farming and property investment. The Duke enjoys shooting and fishing, and spends a lot of time in the estate parklands in his spare time.

ABOVE LEFT The christening of Max, the youngest child of the current Duke and Duchess (then Lord and Lady Ralph Percy), in 1990. Elizabeth, the 10th Duchess, holds Max, with his parents behind; their other children Katie and George stand, while their daughter Melissa sits on the Library carpet.

ABOVE RIGHT The current Duke and Duchess in 2011 at St Michael's Church in Alnwick for the wedding of their eldest daughter, Lady Catherine Percy, to Patrick Valentine.

The Duke is proud of what has been achieved. 'I think it is great what we have done. You know, our first fifteen years have, compared to the preceding three decades, been good for the family. I think it was probably the only opportunity in our lifetime to restore it, and thank God we have done so; otherwise we certainly couldn't start now.'

As well as creating a family home, the Duke and Duchess's key motivation in restoring the castle was to relieve the burden on their eldest son, George, who will inherit the estate, and this they have done. Though he knows he will succeed, George, the Duke says, 'is under no illusion that he has to go out and do his own thing. That is what he wants to do anyway, rather than sit around and wait for me to drop off my perch.' But on the question of succession, the Duke and Duchess share the same views. 'I think, if and when George has children, it would be great to move out and let him take over. We think it is wonderful having children here,' says the Duchess. Were they to move 'early' they would miss the castle, but they are supremely modern on the subject. 'It wouldn't worry us

moving out. I mean, Jane and I have lived in lots of houses throughout our lives,' says the Duke.

'The thing is,' he continues, 'it is so different to a normal house – it is slightly like living in an office sometimes. I emphathized with Deborah, Duchess of Devonshire, when she said at the start of her book on Chatsworth that "we have always lived in furnished rooms". The castle is very special but you never really feel it is your own. It sounds rather corny but you are always looking after it for another generation. It's pass the parcel.' There has been a lot of parcel passing. In 2009, the Duke and Duchess celebrated the 700th anniversary of the Percy family at Alnwick, and hosted a large party for the estate to mark the occasion.

Despite her private pain, Duchess Elizabeth sees the silver lining to the cloud that was her eldest son Harry's premature death. 'When Ralph took over in 1995, everything then grew and developed. Everything has gone terribly well ever since.' Retired agent Mr Hugonin observes that had Ralph not succeeded, 'Jane would not have been functioning at the

castle. And that too would have been a waste of talent for us and the castle.' She is, he says, 'quite remarkable in what she has done. Very, very remarkable.'

Looking back to 1995, Ian August reflects, 'Harry's death was a tragedy for his family. However, in a sense it was a merciful thing from the point of view of the estate that his reign only lasted six years. One does have to say that. Now everything is restored. It is consoling that the Duke's son must now have that comfort, to know the castle is restored.'

FAR LEFT From left to right: the
Duchess, Lord Max, Lady Melissa,
Patrick Valentine, Lady Catherine,
George, Earl Percy, and the Duke in
the State Dining Room.
LEFT George, Earl Percy, and his
younger brother, Lord Max Percy, at
their sister's wedding.
RIGHT The Duchess.

THE STATE ROOMS

ITH ONLY ONE FRONT DOOR, the castle is not designed to be simultaneously both a private home and a tourist attraction. Whereas in an eighteenth-century stately home the family can retreat to one of the wings, at Alnwick this is impossible and it is therefore difficult for the family to have any privacy. So from April to October each year, the family move to Burncastle in the Scottish borders, while they open their home to the public – or the state rooms, to be more precise. 'Two days before the castle opens we pack up, lorries come and we move out,' the Duchess explains. All the signs start going up, the ropes go up, and this place becomes a visitor attraction. It literally takes twenty-four hours when we arrive back here for the winter for it to start feeling like home again.' The following pages describe the public route that visitors follow.

If classic English country house interiors are famous for their 'layers', Alnwick is no exception. Most significant of these layers are the princely Italianate Renaissance-inspired state rooms created by Luigi Canina for the 4th Duke, Algernon, whose total and controversial transformation of the castle in the 1850s and 1860s, in which he employed the architect Anthony Salvin for the exterior and some of the interior, is described on pages 26–9. The state rooms contain the Camuccini Collection of Italian Renaissance Old Masters that the 4th Duke purchased in Rome, and which sit alongside the English and French furniture, paintings and china that he inherited from his brother, parents, grandparents and so on.

The current Duchess updated the castle as a family home for the twenty-first century, at the same time undertaking her enormous conservation project, which began in 1995 and is the other main influence on what visitors see today. This honours the work of both the 4th Duke, Algernon, and another great Percy, the 1st Duchess, Elizabeth Seymour, who turned the family's ruinous castle into a home (as described on pages 20–24).

OPPOSITE The north-facing side of the castle from across the River Aln over James Adam's 1776 Lion Bridge. The windows are, from the left, of the Drawing Room, Saloon and Ante-Library on the ground floor and above of the bedrooms off the Warkworth Corridor. The tallest tower on the right is Salvin's Prudhoe Tower, built as part of the 4th Duke's 1850s transformation and today housing the Family Kitchen, Library and family bedrooms.

ABOVE The entrance into the Keep's inner courtyard is from the 1350 Octagonal Towers, erected by Henry de Percy, 2nd Lord of Alnwick. The family park their cars in here. Inside the arch, on the right-hand side, is the entrance to the dungeon.

THE LOWER GUARD CHAMBER

Salvin's sandstone porte cochère in the courtyard, with its vaulted ceiling, meant that from the 1860s the family could get out of their carriages without being rained on. The stone came from a quarry in Hulne Park.

After passing through the front door, with its enormous seventeenth-century Venetian bronze doorknocker, you arrive in the Lower Guard Chamber, or entrance hall. When the family is in the castle during the shooting period, each guest is allocated a silk-covered chair here, next to which they leave their wellies, and on which they can dump their jackets, scarves and what have you.

The plain masonry walls are covered with the arms of the Percy Tenantry Volunteers, raised by the 2nd Duke during the Napoleonic Wars. Among these hang swords, breastplates and a helmet from the English Civil War. To the right of the doorway is the sword of General Lord Henry Percy, who fought at the Battle of lnkerman in 1854 in the Crimean War and won the Victoria Cross. These were all hung in the early twentieth century. If you want to copy this look, you will need chicken wire, 228 pistols, 523 powder horns, 252 swords, lots of muskets and more.

Through the glass doors is a smaller hall with a white panelled stucco ceiling. This leads to the Grand Staircase. The floor is made of slabs of local stone about 7 feet by 10 feet/ 2 metres by 3 metres, cut so perfectly that you can hardly get your thumbnail between the joins. All the main Victorian heating pipes run underneath it. There are two marble figures,

BELOW LEFT Salvin's porte cochère was added in the early 1860s by the 4th Duke to give the front door protection from the elements and to house the first-floor hall, the Upper Guard Chamber.
BELOW AND RIGHT On display in the Lower Guard Chamber are flintlock Light Dragoon pistols made for the Percy Volunteers in 1800 (below) and the 1st Duke's George III mahogany dining chairs, c.1765 (right).

one called *Action* by John Gott (early nineteenth century), a British sculptor who worked in Rome, and a statue of Louisa, 6th Duchess, by the North American Piers Connolly, from the 1870s. The gilt eagle console table is George II and used to be at Stanwick Hall, one of the 1st Duke's houses in Yorkshire.

Here we see the first sign of Charles Hesp, a decorative painter who trained under John Fowler and is renowned for his painted decoration in St Paul's Cathedral; his work is in evidence throughout the castle. 'I started working with Charles after I saw what he had done at Arundel,' explains the Duchess. 'He is a top Adam specialist, a fine decorative painter, and he commissions and hangs our silks for the state rooms. We work on the colours together. I will say to him, "What are we going to do here?" and he will come up with several ideas. I know what he has done has been right every time. That is worth everything – to have people you really trust and respect.' At the foot of the Grand Staircase you can see Hesp's *trompe-l'oeil* marble, created as he and the Duchess wanted to bring the look of the staircase walls down into this hall at the foot of the stairs.

PREVIOUS PAGES A group of 160 1796 Pattern Light Cavalry Troopers' swords of the Percy Volunteers, 228 flintlock Light Dragoon pistols and 523 powder horns of cow horn and brass decorate the 1860s Lower Guard Chamber. The design follows an earlier sketch by the 2nd Duke of a display that he saw in Lexington during the American War of Independence.

BELOW LEFT To this day, the Duke of Northumberland donates and drops the ball for the annual football match that has taken place since 1762 in the pastures beneath Alnwick Castle on Shrove Tuesday. In this 1828 notice Alnwick's Town Commissioners banned 'Foot-ball in the Streets'.

BELOW RIGHT The castle's visitors' books include the signatures of the Queen, Prince Philip, French president Giscard D'Estaing and the King of Spain.

RIGHT Through the Victorian glass doors of the Lower Guard Chamber there is a smaller hall before the Grand Staircase.

PAGES 52 AND 53 The marble candelabras flanking the hall before the Grand Staircase were made in the Roman workshops of Montiroli. The console table with eagle is George II with a peach marble top, attributed to Henry Flitcroft. It was at the 1st Duke's Stanwick Hall in Yorkshire, and then Albury, the Surrey estate, before coming to Alnwick.

THE GRAND STAIRCASE

The first taste of magnificence inside the castle can be had from looking up the 1861 Grand Staircase. The walls blend Carrara marble with a groin-vaulted ceiling with foliated stucco ornament by Taccolozzi. The marble balustrade and candelabra flanking the staircase were made in the Roman workshops of Giovanni Montiroli.

The carpet on the stairs takes a pounding. After one year when over 250,000 visitors walked up, around and back down again it was decided that visitors should exit elsewhere. Ian August explains: 'The original carpet put in by the 4th Duke

was worn and tatty. It wasn't so much an issue from the family point of view but they realized that there might be insurance implications if they left it in place. We checked the records and found the company who had made and laid the carpet in the mid-nineteenth century, and they told us, "We still have the measurements."' So they made new ones.

Each step of the staircase is a single piece of stone, 12 feet/3.5 metres long, from a local quarry at Rothbury. The landing halfway up consists of a single stone 12 feet/ 3.5 metres square. The pale blue silk and gilt sofa at the top of the stairs is English and George III. There are some recent family portraits here, but these are best seen from the top of the stairs in the Upper Guard Chamber.

THE UPPER GUARD CHAMBER

This loggia-style hall, 30 feet/9 metres square, is part of Salvin's new structure, added to the castle in the mid-nineteenth century. Austere, lofty and 'chaste', it is meant to be Italianate, although you will notice not only that the paintings are mostly English but that the furniture is English too – Georgian. The armchairs are by John Linnell, and the grand gilt table under Claude's *Sunset*, and the one under the

10th Duke's portrait, are George II. The pair under the figures of *Justice* and *Britannia* in the alcoves are George I.

The Upper Guard Chamber was redecorated in 1999 and was one of the Duchess's first state room decorative projects. It is a walk-through area but the Duke's piper uses it before grand dinners and it is where the Christmas tree stands each December. Previously the walls were a cold pale grey-blue colour but they are now closer to the original, a beige sandy colour. Charles Hesp redid the ceiling by introducing different shades of white, and with the alternating lighter and darker tones the decoration and detail gain depth.

High on the walls are frieze panels, as in Roman palazzos. But here they represent scenes from the Battle of Chevy Chase. The 1st Duchess's chaplain published the ballad 'Chevy Chase' in the *Ancient Reliques of English Poetry* in the 1760s: this tells of the legendary bloody battle between the Percys and the Dowager Duchess Elizabeth's Douglas ancestors. The artist

Francis Gotzenberg was pushed to complete the four scenes on the panels in a year and half. However, his patron, the 4th Duke, died before seeing them all finished. More recently the four oil-on-canvas friezes, which are 7 feet/2 metres high and 13 feet/4 metres long, suffered severe water damage, so they went off for a three-year-long conservation holiday. The Duke complains, 'We did improve the lighting in here but you still can't see them properly.'

Canina stipulated a marble floor and after he died in 1856, his assistant, Giovanni Montiroli, took over, and designed the marble mosaic floor in the Venetian style, inspired by the Temple of Hadrian in Rome. The crack in the floor is due to historic settlement. Building surveyor Robin Smeaton, who spends his time looking after the major heritage assets on the estate, explains: 'We are above the main entrance here, so there has been a relaxation of Salvin's structure. The majority of Alnwick is built on sand, but the footings are massive, so at foundation level all of this massive weight is being spread across a huge area.'

The 26-foot/8-metre-high ceilings are in stucco, inspired by the Italian Renaissance. The arches and groins of the staircase, panel mouldings and pier arches dividing the chamber from the staircase carry foliate designs which continue into the Upper Guard Chamber ceiling. The chandelier is William IV. It was once a gas chandelier and the gas pipes remain inside.

Other items in here include a bronze head of Winston Churchill by Verbon, made in 1953, and, on the table beneath a Claude Lorraine painting (*Sunset*, 1637), a Chinese Ming-dynasty large 'Compagnies des Indes' christening bowl of the Jiajing period. On the tables beneath *Justice* and *Britannia* are two late sixteenth-century blue and white Chinese Kraak Ming porcelain bowls of the Wanli period.

This hall houses many important paintings in the collection, as well as the most recent portraits of the Percy family. One of these is of George, the current Duke and Duchess's eldest son, when he was pageboy to the Queen in 1995 by Katrina Bovill; others are of the Duke's father, Duke Hugh, as Master of the Percy Foxhounds, and of his mother, Duchess Elizabeth, on the moor, both painted by Oswald Birley in 1946/7; and a portrait

LEFT A 1953 bronze head of Sir Winston Churchill by Verbon sits by the window.
RIGHT This lofty loggia-style hall above the entrance is a central part of Salvin's mid-nineteenth-century innovations to the layout. The mosaic floor was inspired by the Italian Temple of Hadrian, although you will notice that the paintings and furniture are mostly English. The chandelier is William IV.

LEFT As in Roman palazzos, the hall has frieze panels beneath the ceiling. These represent scenes from the Battle of Chevy Chase, fought between the Percys and the Douglases, ancestors of the Dowager Duchess Elizabeth. Each is 7 x 13 feet/2 x 4 metres and took Francis Gotzenberg a year and half to paint, but the 4th Duke died in 1865 before seeing them all finished. The current Duchess recently had them restored, which took three years.

OPPOSITE

ABOVE LEFT Painted at Alnwick in 1946 by Oswald Birley, a portrait of the Duke's father, the 10th Duke, who first opened the castle to the public in 1950.

ABOVE CENTRE The Duke's mother, 10th Duchess, Dowager Duchess Elizabeth, painted by Oswald Birley in 1947, made few changes in the castle, knowing her husband simply wanted to keep a hunt going, have a good shoot and make sure that the tenants were happy. 'Horrified' at first sight, she made the castle cosy and was very happy here.

ABOVE RIGHT A portrait painted posthumously by Oswald Birley, of the bachelor Henry, 9th Duke, who died fighting the Nazis in 1940, thrusting his brother, the Duke's father, into the position of 10th Duke.

BELOW Above the Grand Staircase hangs a portrait of Helen, 8th Duchess, by Philip de László, in her 1937 coronation robes and wearing the Northumberland strawberry-leaf tiara. After George VI's death she remained Mistress of the Robes to Queen Elizabeth the Queen Mother until 1964.

FOLLOWING PAGES

LEFT Helen, 8th Duchess, daughter of the 7th Duke of Richmond, painted in 1916 by Philip de László when she was married, at twenty-nine years old, and two years before her husband, Alan Percy, succeeded as 8th Duke. The giltwood sofa is 1825.

RIGHT London in 1747, seen through an arch of Westminster Bridge, by Canaletto. commissioned by Sir Hugh Smithson, later the 1st Duke, who was one of the commissioners of the bridge. The current Duke says guests like this Canaletto more than any other in the castle. The George III chair is part of a set commissioned from Linnell by the 1st Duke for Syon House.

of the Duke's elder brother, Harry, the 11th Duke, painted posthumously by Andrew Festing in 1997 is here. There is also one of the Duke's uncle, Henry George, the 9th Duke, who was killed in Belgium during the retreat to Dunkirk in the Second World War. It was painted from a photograph, again by Oswald Birley, in 1947 and was said to be a good likeness.

The most dominant painting in the room is 'of Granny': Philip de László's ravishing portrait of the Duke's grandmother, Helen, 8th Duchess, a statuesque beauty, painted in 1916 during the First World War. There is a second de László portrait of her as Mistress of the Robes to Queen Elizabeth at the coronation of George VI in 1937 above the Grand Staircase. You can see that she decided to break the rules by taking off the coronet and putting it on the table. She liked her tiaras, wearing them throughout her life; in the 1950s one was snatched by a thief outside her house in Eaton Square before a state dinner at Buckingham Palace.

In this room are also three Italian paintings from the Camuccini Collection. Claude Lorraine's *Sunset* (1637) was painted for Pope Urban VII. 'About twenty years ago this was incredibly dirty – you could hardly see anything,' says Duke Ralph. 'After it was cleaned they discovered that this chap has a pair of spectacles on. When I was growing up, the theory was that one of father's generation, one of my aunts, had painted them on for fun but later they went right back to the original paint and discovered that the spectacles are original.' The second from the Camuccini Collection is *The Blind Leading the Blind*, studio of Domenico Feti, *c.*1600, and the third is *Infancy Crowning Death*, *c.*1520, by Lorenzo Lotto, which the Duke describes as 'spooky'.

The hall also holds the castle's first Van Dyck on show (early seventeenth century), of Algernon, 10th Earl, beautifully captured at the court of Charles l. A patron of Van Dyck and Peter Lely, this earl collected Old Masters such as Titian and started the Percy art collection.

On the same wall in the Upper Guard Chamber are the castle's most popular Canalettos. One is of Syon House, painted in 1749, one of the Old Westminster Bridge under construction, and one of Windsor Castle as it looked in 1747. The fourth, *London Seen Through an Arch of Westminster Bridge*, with a bucket hanging from the bridge, the 1st Duke commissioned in 1747 as he was helping to organize the building of the bridge. 'Funnily enough, most people say if they could have any of the Canalettos in the house they would have that one,' the Duke says.

LEFT Claude Lorrain's *Sunset* was painted for Pope Urban VII in 1637. The 4th Duke acquired it with the Camuccini Collection in 1856 to complement his Italianate interiors. Under the painting, on a George II console table, is a sixteenth-century Chinese Ming dynasty christening bowl.

ABOVE Four of the 1st Duke's Canalettos hang in the Upper Guard Chamber. These three are, clockwise from left, of Windsor Castle in 1747, painted from the 1st Duchess's grandfather's Percy Lodge; of the Northumberlands' Syon House by the Thames, 1749; and of the old Westminster Bridge, 1746/7.

THE ANTE-LIBRARY

This is a walk-through room, used by the butler to make cocktails when the family are next door in the Library.

When these photographs were taken, this room had yet to be refurbished by the Duchess. The ceiling will be cleaned to get rid of over 150 years of grime. A rug will replace the wall-to-wall carpet. Ian August says, 'The idea is that we can lift and turn a rug, so the wear can be spread. After a lot of research we realized that protective mats laid over carpet exacerbates problems: the accumulating dirt between the two layers accelerates carpet wear. Now you allow people to walk on the carpet and just have a very robust cleaning regime in place.'

The photographs don't show the crystal chandelier either, as it was being restored after a recent calamity. The Duchess picks up the story: 'We try to conserve and repair one room every two years. And the chandelier crashed down when it was being cleaned. It took the whole budget of one year.' After the crash, Ian August explains, they also found that 'The way they had been hung in the past, partly threaded, had quietly been unthreading over decades. We needed to strengthen the support cabling and chains, and installed a double security.'

Originally, the Ante-Library was hung in green Milanese silk, which was replaced early in the twentieth century with this pretty blue Colefax and Fowler wall silk. The ceiling is carved

in pine and painted and gilded, while the dado is inlaid with sycamore. The ceiling and dado show off the craftsmanship of the Alnwick School of Carving, set up by the 4th Duke in the 1850s to supply local carvers to work alongside the Italian craftsmen. The chimneypiece by Giovanni Taccalozzi is of white marble and red oriental granite, with figures executed by Nucci. On top are pieces of 1825 Royal Worcester china. The Duchess puts some of her recent books on two round marquetry tables that the 3rd Duke bought in 1823 from Morel and Hughes for £18.

Luckily, the paintings were unaffected by the crashing chandelier. Here is another big purchase by the 4th Duke, from the Manfrini Gallery in Venice, including *The Lady with the Lute* by Palma Vecchio (*c*.1520), *The Artist and his Pupils* by Bernardino Licinio (*c*.1500) and Titian's *Bishop and his Secretary* (1537), part of the 10th Earl's collection of Old Masters. Alongside it is another Titian, *Ecce Homo* (mid-1500s).

The Titianesque group of Italian Old Masters here is intended to complement the Italian cinquecento-style interiors the 4th Duke favoured. Perhaps the most famous is *Portrait of a Man with his Wife and Son* (*c*.1500), which Lord Byron viewed in the Manfrini Gallery in 1817 and praised in his poem 'Beppo': 'That picture (howsoever fine the rest)/Is loveliest to my mind of all the show . . . 'Tis but a portrait of his son and wife,/And self; but such a Woman! Love in Life!'

On either side of the door into the Library hang large framed fragments of an amazing Renaissance fresco, *The Visitation* painted by Sebastiano del Piombo and believed to have been drawn by Michelangelo. It was painted on the walls of the Santa Maria della Pace in Rome, *c*.1530.

ABOVE Clockwise from top left, all sixteenth century: Palma Vecchio's *Lady with a Lute*; Licinio's *The Artist and his Pupils*; *Portrait of a Man with his Wife and Son*, after Titian; *A Portrait of a Bearded Man*, after Titian; Titian's *Bishop and his Secretary*, of Georges d'Armagnac and his secretary Philandrier.

RIGHT The chimneypiece figures are nineteenth century by Nucci; the giltwood mirror was designed by Montiroli in the 1850s; the round tables were made in 1823 for the 3rd Duke.

THE LIBRARY

Like many rooms at Alnwick this one has been put to many uses. It is now the family's main sitting room. Best at night with roaring fires and scented by candles, it is my favourite room in the castle, and perhaps one of the best in England.

It is remarkably cosy, despite taking one whole floor of Salvin's Prudhoe Tower, measuring 56 feet/17 metres in length and with ceilings 23 feet/7 metres high. There are a staggering 14,500 books here, dating from about 1475.

The 9th Earl assembled one of the finest Renaissance libraries in England, which helped keep him amused during his many years locked up in the Tower of London. His son Algernon was educated at the Tower and added to the collection. The 1st Duchess Elizabeth's mother, Frances, Duchess of Somerset, bought numerous items. So each generation has made its contribution: the 3rd Duke was keen on gardening; the fifth on Spain; the sixth on religion and so on. The 7th Duke had antiquarian interests and the Duke's father, the 10th Duke, collected himself and went some way in putting back together the collection of the 9th 'Tower of London' or 'Wizard' Earl.

Even in winter, the temperature inside the castle is warm. The Duke explains, 'It has to be kept at a constant temperature for the sake of the books. I think leather dries out otherwise, so the humidity and warmth are carefully controlled. There is a whopping great heating bill but having the American University in part of the castle helps to defray the cost. Heating is just one of those things you have got to keep doing.'

If the Duke is now a careful conservationist he was not always so. 'I came back from Oxford with a keg of beer that I had been given for Christmas. I left it on the bookcase here and forgot about it. About three weeks later, I was back at Oxford when the thing exploded. I wasn't very popular.'

Pencil and crayon drawings of the Duke's family are dotted around the bookshelves at waist height. Some were done in 1965 by Molly Bishop, others later by her daughter Charmian Campbell, and the most recent ones of the current family by Nicholas Beer in 2003.

Italian architect Giovanni Montiroli designed the Library

LEFT Built in 1854, the 4th Duke's Library occupies the whole of the first floor of the Prudhoe Tower and houses 14,500 books on light oak bookshelves, the earliest of which dates from the late fifteenth century. Like many items in the castle, the 1822 chandelier came from Northumberland House, on Trafalgar Square, which was demolished in 1874.

ABOVE Marble bust of Sir Isaac Newton by Giovanni Strazza, c.1860, which, with busts of William Shakespeare and Francis Bacon, decorates the Library's three Siena, Africanos and white marble chimneypieces.
RIGHT Giovanni Montiroli's designs for the coffered panels of the Library ceiling have trophies representing the 4th Duke's interest in art, music, archaeology, the navy and, shown here, science, technology and astronomy.

for the 4th Duke. The bookshelves are in light oak, inlaid with sycamore. Reflecting the 4th Duke's passions, the ceiling is divided into compartments in which are coffered panels with carved trophies designed by Montiroli representing Art, Music and the Sciences. The fourth is dedicated to archaeology and the navy. The Alnwick School of Carving made the ceiling under the supervision of a Florentine master carver, Anton Bulletti. The 4th Duke, a naval man, also put in a coastal weather station complete with clock, barometer and weather gauges by Negretti and Zambra in 1860.

The three fireplaces were designed by Taccalozzi in Siena and Africanos inlaid in white marble. They are decorated with marble busts of Francis Bacon, Isaac Newton and William Shakespeare.

The wall-to-wall carpet is from Walt Disney, indirectly. Having tripped on the old carpet, the Duke's mother, the Dowager Duchess Elizabeth, 'made a scene' and persuaded her husband to use the money from the filming of *King Arthur* at Alnwick to pay for this St Cuthbert's Cross carpet made by McKays of Durham.

The curtains weigh a ton and were designed by the interior designer Lucy Manners; they were installed in 2004 by the London upholsterer and curtain-maker Thomson-Shultz Ltd. 'Through my lifetime there weren't any – perhaps only some rather nasty brown things up there which were never shut,' explains the Duke. The Duchess adds, 'You can't mess around with a room like this but you can enhance it. You had the exterior lights of the castle shining through the windows. So the first thing we wanted to do when we could afford to was to put up the curtains.' The fabric was designed by the interior designer Robert Kime and is also used on the gilt chairs.

Much of the furniture was ordered in the 1820s for Northumberland House, such as the giltwood armchairs by Morel and Hughes, the pair of rosewood and marquetry library writing tables and the chandelier. However, the Duchess prefers not to use the chandelier. 'Lighting is an obsession of mine, indoors and outdoors. I think it subconsciously affects your mood. I hate light shining in on you. I will never have on an overhead light if I can have a side lamp on. Luckily, there

LEFT Effectively the drawing room, the Library is 56 feet/17 metres long and 23 feet/7 metres high, yet this favourite room is both grand and curiously cosy, especially in the evening, when drinks are served and the Duchess's scented candles are lit.

were plenty of lamps here when we moved in.'

Two paintings here worth looking at are the seventeenth-century *Erminia and the Shepherds* by Sisto Badalocchio (mid-1600s) and *Bacchus and Ariadne*, attributed to Poussin, a copy of a Titian which hangs in the National Gallery.

Lastly, it must be said that the room is beautifully scented. 'I have always got candles burning,' says the Duchess. 'I don't like fragrances which are too sweet – I like fruits and woody scents but I don't like musk. We vary the candles a bit.'

Photographs of the Duke and Duchess's children sit around the room and the TV. The Duchess elaborates: 'Houses, I feel, are really sensitive to atmosphere. You can feel in some properties which are not lived in that they lack the atmosphere that a proper house should have. I like to leave things around in the Library so visitors can feel that a family has been here. Perhaps some of our silly Christmas stocking gifts, Voodoo dolls or whatever.' The room also has some of the Duchess's stuffed dogs, squirrels and birds.

THE SALOON

Unlike the Library this room is rarely used, except for receptions or when the family play ping-pong after dinner. 'I love the rooms but they are nothing without people in them. I don't want to sit in a beautiful room on my own and look around it and think, Isn't this beautiful?' says the Duchess.

The room used to be the music room and the Duke recalls, 'My mother used to come and play her piano in here and we would have music lessons and the Christmas tree in here. I have memories of standing beside the tree with a sponge on the end of a stick and having to dab out the candles. I don't think anybody ever sat or chatted in here, even Duchess Louise. It was very similar to what it is now.'

This 'jewel box' of a room has the French and Italian atmosphere of an Englishman's Grand Tour. On the double doors carved central bosses in walnut depict Medusa heads. Taccalozzi in Rome carved the fireplace, which has figurative 6-foot/1.75-metre-tall Dacian slaves by Nucci, all in the best Carrara marble; models in gesso were sent to the Duke for his approval first. The fireplace looks as if it was directly copied from the one in the Quirinal Palace in the Sala del Thorwaldsen. Vivid turquoise-blue Sèvres vases adorn the fireplace and the ebony Boulle furniture was made in Paris specifically for this room. Overhead is a painted and gilded ceiling that rivals any Roman fifteenth- or sixteenth-century palace: it could not be more Renaissance.

There are also four glorious Canalettos, two of highly atmospheric Venetian street landscapes, another showing Northumberland House, every inch one's 'town palazzo', and fourthly the derelict Alnwick Castle just before the renovations of the 1st Duke and Duchess. The Duke wonders 'whether Canaletto ever came up here or whether it is just done from other people's sketches. It is out of perspective, particularly the figures on the hillside.'

The room is also adorned with portraits by Lely, Gascars, Van Dyck, and William Dobson, who is believed by many to

LEFT The influence of the cinquecento Italian design in the castle is at its fullest in the ceilings, fireplaces, window shutters, frieze and, seen here, lion door details of the Saloon.

RIGHT The 1st Duke's Canaletto, of a corner of Piazza San Marco in Venice, was painted in 1740 and came from Stanwick Hall in 1922, to hang above one of the room's four Boulle cabinets, commissioned by his grandson, the 4th Duke, from Paris. The room was extensively restored in 2008. The Duchess introduced curtains to complement the new wall silks, which are exact copies of the original 1864 Milanese damask from Ambrosio Osnago.

RIGHT Northumberland House in 1752 by Canaletto. This fine town house in Trafalgar Square was knocked down by Act of Parliament in 1874 to expand the square, but if standing today would be seen from the steps of the National Gallery. The statue of Charles I on horseback remains.

BELOW Including works by Lely, Tisi, Van Dyck and Canaletto, the paintings in the Saloon alone indicate what must be one of the most valuable private art collections in the country. William Dobson's portrait of three cavaliers is one of the greatest paintings in the collection, the current Duke says. Painted in the 1640s, it shows Nicholas Lanier, Dobson himself in red and Sir Charles Cotterell, after the end of the Civil War. Some consider Dobson to be the most important English artist before Hogarth.

OPPOSITE The Saloon's Italianate chimneypiece, with two statues of Dacian prisoners by Nucci, looks similar to one at the Quirinal Palace in Rome in the Sala del Thorwaldsen. As in Roman palazzos, the state rooms at Alnwick have painted friezes beneath the cornice under the ceiling; this one is by Alessandro Mantovani. The grand furniture the 3rd Duke commissioned for Northumberland House included these 1823 chairs and sofas from Morel and Hughes, which Robert Kime recently reupholstered.

be the most important English artist before Hogarth. The Dobson is one of the greatest paintings in the collection. The Duke says it was 'painted in the 1640s – it is three cavaliers, Nicholas Lanier, Dobson himself and Sir Charles Cotterell, after the end of the Civil War drowning their sorrows'.

Apart from paintings from the Camuccini Collection, many of the portraits here pay homage to the family's seventeenth-century royal and Percy ancestors. These include the French wife of Charles I, Queen Henrietta Maria, painted by Sir Anthony Van Dyck. Both the Duke's mother, Elizabeth, and his grandmother, Helen, descend from this marriage via Henrietta Maria's son Charles II. Henri Gascars's portrait of Elizabeth Percy, Duchess of Somerset, is a reminder of the Duke's link to the 1066 Percys, through her inheritance of the Percy estates in 1670. Her parents, the 11th Earl of Northumberland and his countess, are both here too, to the right of the chimneypiece, painted by Lely. And the 10th Earl reappears too, again painted by Van Dyck.

The room's Italian Renaissance character is striking in the ceilings, fireplaces, doors, window shutters and friezes here. As the castle's 'guide for the guides' explains: 'The design of the ceiling was suggested by decorations in St Peter's in Rome and the frieze, in brightly rich arabesques on a dark blue ground, was painted in Rome by Alessandro Mantovani, one of the important artists engaged in the 1840s decoration of the Vatican. Although by fame Mantovani was the most prominent of all the Italian artists employed in Alnwick's

restoration, his studio confined its work to the friezes which decorate the Saloon and Drawing Room. They were painted in oil on canvas and mounted on frames to fit the shape of the room . . . The frieze design is in imitation of the work of Raphael.'

The very English super-grand part-1750s chandelier is made up of over 1,800 pieces and was designed to take twenty-five candles. Its cut-glass droppers and necklaces were added

later. This light is one of three that hung in the ballroom in Northumberland House, now all at Alnwick. The design is the same as the one that crashed in the Ante-Library next door, and the third hangs next door in the Drawing Room.

The massive mirror's gilt frame was designed by Montiroli in the 1860s. The room is interesting for its French Boulle-style furniture, and the pair of cabinets designed and ordered from Paris by the 4th Duke for this room on either side of

LEFT On the 1680s Louis XIV commode is a divine early eighteenth-century Boulle clock by Bastien of Paris, next to a framed photo of the Dowager Duchess Elizabeth. She used to play the piano in the Saloon, when it was called the Music Room. Above the clock is a portrait of a man by Annibale Carracci, of the Bolognese School, c.1600, part of the Camuccini Collection.
ABOVE A detail of one of the Boulle cabinets. This Louis XIV-inspired style is decidedly foreign, and might be too grand for some English country houses, but it suits this room and is totally evocative of a ducal Grand Tour.

the doors. There is also a pair of premier contre-partie Boulle tables either side of the fireplace. This Louis XIV style, with its fancy inlay in either tortoiseshell or brass against ebony wood and gold mounts, might be too grand for many English country houses, but here it is evocative of a ducal Grand Tour.

Next to the windows is a pair of Louis XIV commodes. On one is a divine early eighteenth-century clock by Bastien of Paris, again in a Boulle case, and on the other, right, stands a historic but not very attractive small inlaid drawer cabinet presented to Duchess Helen by George V and Queen Mary in 1924.

Made to impress, the stately set of gilt chairs, sofas and stools are English and part of a suite commissioned by the 3rd Duke in 1823 by Morel and Hughes for Northumberland House. They were originally covered in crimson damask, but the Duchess had the suite re-gilded in 1997 and reupholstered, using Robert Kime to design a new fabric in a red and gold stripe.

The room was restored in 2008, as Robin Smeaton explains. 'The ceiling was cleaned. All of the artwork was taken off site to be conserved.' And the huge mirror? 'I am afraid we chickened out with the mirrors. Look at the size of the mirror and then at the size of the door cases. The mirrors must have come in before the door cases were put in. So the mirror was conserved *in situ*.'

The silk walls are new. 'The quality and pattern were matched with the original silk. Although this is not from Ambrosio Osnago of Milan what you see now is a copy, sewn at the Humphries Weaving Co. Ltd of Suffolk.' Charles Hesp hung the silk using steam. In the process the humidity caused the newly restored metal fire surround to oxidize. 'There was a little bit of a learning curve there,' admits Robin Smeaton. The Duchess's conservation programme included the cleaning of the woodwork, floor, fireplace, marble mantle and surround. A new rug carpet was laid, designed by a Welsh company, D. & S. Bamford Ltd. New curtains and blinds were hung, all the pictures were cleaned and the room was rewired.

The Duchess occasionally ponders on the conservation. 'In a way I am not sure if it is good or bad. I sometimes go into the rooms we have just done and you wouldn't know we had done them. I think, Does anybody know it took two years of hard work to get this room right? My mother-in-law went into this room and I said, "Elizabeth, come and look." And she looked and she said, "Yes?" I said, "Well, we have done it up – we have used the same silk on the walls, made a brand-new carpet." She had no idea at first.'

THE DRAWING ROOM

The restoration of this room started in 2008 and finished in 2009, and was done in exactly the same way as the Saloon. It cost £200,000. The room is designed to be the most sumptuous in the castle, but aside from it being 46 feet/14 metres long, I think the smaller Saloon almost equals it in splendour. I say almost, for a pair of exquisite cabinets makes this room the winner.

The cabinets on either side of the fireplace are among the most rare and expensive pieces of furniture in the entire world. Louis XIV of France commissioned them from his Gobelins factory for his palace of Versailles in about 1683. Made by Domenico Cucci from ebony, marble and bronze gilt and covered with semi-precious stones including amethysts and lapis lazuli, they are examples of the most opulent surviving pieces of furniture from the Baroque era, and some of the only surviving furniture from Louis XIV's Versailles.

It is no surprise that the Duke calls these 'The best of the best. They are by far the most valuable items in the collection

LEFT The Domenico Cucci cabinets on either side of the fireplace were made for Louis XIV, and purchased in 1822 by the acquisitive 3rd Duke. Perhaps the most expensive pieces of Baroque furniture in the world, they sit quite happily in the castle's grandest room.

ABOVE A detail of the *pietra dura*-decorated Cucci cabinets.

here. Although, to my taste they look a bit gaudy.' Gaudy or not, he is keeping them. 'President Giscard of France was once shooting here. Every time he passed for dinner he would sigh, shake his head and say, "They should be in Paris, Versailles." I think he was under the impression that they had been looted.' They were not. Records found from the French royal accounts for Versailles prove that they were sold by the French state in 1751. The furniture then disappeared until 1822, when the 3rd Duke bought them for Northumberland House when he was Ambassador to France. However, the Duke sent one cabinet back on a short trip to Versailles for an exhibition in 2011.

The latest research on the decorative motifs of gardens, flowers and animals strongly suggests they were made for the private apartments at Versailles of Louis XIV's mistress, Madame de Montespan. Her apartments at the palace were filled with pet animals and flowers; the King's apartments show that he liked more masculine or military motifs. His mistress, whose full name was Françoise de Rochechouart de Mortemart, Marchioness of Montespan, was so influential that she was dubbed 'the real Queen'. She not only gave the King seven children but also apparently poisoned any woman at court who threatened her control over the *saucisson-imperiale*. Most of the drawers and compartments have locks, probably for Madame's jewellery or poisons. 'They were easier to open before they were restored. Now they are quite tricky to get into,' says the Duchess. The doors of the cabinet are covered in semi-precious stones in *pietra dura*.

The ebonized cabinet by the door to the Dining Room displays the ivories the 1st Duchess bought on her travels to the Continent in the 1760s and 1770s. Each depicts hunting or peasant scenes inspired by Dutch artists of the seventeenth century. The 1st Duchess's journal says these were carved by a 'Servant of the late Elector of Cologne'. On one table is her charming French 1740s bridal fan. Her journal also records that she paid £12 for *Orpheus Attacked by the Thracian Women* by Frans Francken the Younger, Kierincx and Savery (pre-1626), which hangs here. After the 1822 alterations to Northumberland House during the reign of George IV (once the Prince Regent), the 3rd Duke commissioned Morel and Hughes to refit the interiors, which included the making of the 1823 gilt sofas and chairs here. The Duchess moved the 1st Duke's set of Louis XIV-style chairs to the Boudoir corridor and elsewhere.

Now picture perfect, what is curious about this room is that little of the furniture was originally here immediately after it was built in the 1860s. Nor, if you read Luigi Canina's interior plan of 1856, do you see much thought, if any, put into the furniture. In the middle of Victoria's reign, however, the 4th

Duke, Algernon, commissioned the large round 'Five Senses' table with marquetry. It took so long to make that the Duke died before it arrived at the castle. It is extraordinary in its way, but has hideous clumpy legs. Most of the furniture, including the Louis XIV cabinets, predates the interior and came from Northumberland House, after the 4th Duke had died. After Northumberland House was demolished in 1874, the Percys probably did not know what else to do with all the stately stuff from London – which is why there is another gigantic ballroom-sized chandelier here, as in the Saloon.

Perhaps the 4th Duke was more interested in showing off his *tour de force* of Old Masters, fourteen of them from the Camuccini Collection. They include *Portrait of a Young Man* by Andrea del Sarto (early sixteenth century), *The*

ABOVE A fan owned by the exuberant, jolly and acquisitive 1st Duchess, who amassed a vast collection of curiosities, now sadly much dispersed.

RIGHT Some of the 1st Duchess's important collection of ivories are on view here, on an 1820s ebonized and gilt display cabinet commissioned by the 3rd Duke to house them. The ivories are decorated with Low Country peasant scenes of merry-making in the seventeenth-century Dutch style, after Teniers and Ostade, and fanciful hunting scenes after Philips Wouwermans.

LEFT TO RIGHT Roman caryatids by Nucci decorate the Drawing Room's marble chimneypiece; Charles Hesp rehung the new wall silks when the room was entirely restored in 2008–9; the carving of each pair of limewood window shutters took a year of a craftsman's time in the 1850s.

Crucifixion by Guido Reni (1625/6), *The Holy Family* by Giorgio Vasari (1540s), and two paintings by Sisto Badalocchio (early seventeenth century). A leaf of a diptych, *Coronation of the Virgin* and *Scenes from the Life of St John, Catherine and Francis*, is the oldest piece of art in the castle, made *c*.1305 by an Umbrian and one of the three Rimini brothers, Giovanni; they formed the Rimini school. All alone is the Percys' only painting by J.M.W. Turner, our famous English painter, *View of the Temple of Jupiter Panhellenios* (1816) – actually the Temple of Afea on the island of Aegina – reflecting the 4th Duke's passion for archaeology. Sympathetic to Greek independence from the Turks, Turner painted the Greek National Dance of the Romaika and, further away, the Acropolis of Athens.

Montiroli designed a symmetrical gold ceiling using a honeycomb of crosses, octagons and elongated hexagons. Alessandro Mantovani painted the frieze of the Drawing Room in oil on canvas. The frieze bears a design of putti, medallions and classical heads in the style used by Guilio Romano for the sixteenth-century decoration of the Castello di Angelo in Rome. The walls were covered with red silk damask ornamented in a gold pattern, below which is a dado of mahogany with walnut and bird's-eye maple marquetry panels. The double doors are embellished with foliate decoration in walnut with central bosses of Medusa heads. The chimneypiece, of carved Carrara marble, is again by Taccalozzi with figures by Nucci.

Those interested in china should know that the room displays a variety of plates or figurines from Sèvres, Nantgarw, Swansea, Frankenthal, Ludwigsburg, Chelsea-Derby and Meissen. The vase on the centre of the chimneypiece is the most important, being of the Chinese Qing Dynasty Kangxi period. There are a dish and basin near the windows, both of which are Qing Dynasty from the Qianlong period.

THE STATE DINING ROOM

After the Library, this is the Duchess's favourite state room. 'I love this room. It is at its best when it is buzzing and full of people. When you see it being used properly, or you have a shooting party or our daughter's wedding in 2011, and you see the State Dining Room with flowers everywhere, the fires lit, it is magical.'

Canina's plan for this room in 1856 hints at his relief in having, at last, straight lines in which to work the ceiling. 'The rectangle form of this room offers a good opportunity for regular divisions,' he writes. 'The ceiling will be carved and left with the natural tint of the wood.' He then prescribes the rest. 'The colour of the damask for the walls to be carmine red. In the centre of the long side of this room a large marble chimney-piece, composed of two figures, adapted from the most celebrated works of the ancients, but varying with the other chimney-pieces.' And so on. Today it looks almost exactly as he intended, except the silk is green after its restoration and conservation.

Ian August describes how the room was when he started

OPPOSITE This cinquecento-style ceiling, 46 x 34 feet/14 x 10 metres, is the most splendid in the castle – indeed in Britain. The room's irregular shape tested the skills of the designer Giovanni Montiroli. During the Duchess's 2008–9 restoration of the Drawing Room it took five specialists five weeks to clean the ceiling.

ABOVE LEFT Turner's *View of the Temple of Jupiter Panhellenios*, 1816, acquired by the 4th Duke. His friend Charles Cockerell excavated what is more accurately called the Temple of Afea on the island of Aegina with Otto Magnus von Stackelberg in 1811. Athens is in the far distance.

ABOVE RIGHT *Francesco Maria II della Rovere, Duke of Urbino* by the studio of Federico Barocci, late sixteenth century.

RIGHT Removing the 1st Duchess's Robert Adam interiors, the 4th Duke wanted his 1850s renovations to be in the Italian style of the fifteenth and sixteenth centuries. In fact the State Dining Room feels padded and woody compared to the orgiastic use of *trompe-l'oeil* and colourful marbles found in Rome, but better suits this great baronial castle. The 1856 design had carmine-red damask, but when the room was extensively restored in 2006, the Duchess introduced – to acclaim – green damask for the walls and, as in the Saloon and Drawing Room, a new carpet. The room is used throughout the autumn and winter.

working for the Duke's father in 1955. 'It had a burgundy colour on it. The silk in Duke Hugh's time was in a terrible state and he agreed that we do something. It was too expensive to put silk on, so we put fake suede on the walls, which did work to a certain extent.'

But after 1995 the Duchess decided a fresh look was needed. She explains how they came to the green silk. 'My mother-in-law changed it and the walls became a sort of orangey-coppery crushed velvet-suede. I got rid of that. There was also a brown carpet – it wasn't really a carpet, it was like a mat. But I found a green cushion in a bedroom that was the most beautiful vibrant green. People told me that if I did dark green it could make people look yellow or ill, but this was such a beautiful green that I just couldn't believe it. Yet I was worried, so I did quite a lot of research on the right green. I love green. There are greens and greens. It now works beautifully, but mostly because you are using it at night, during the winter with the fire lit. If you were to use this room during the day I think it wouldn't be right.' To my eye, the room looks rather wonderful even in the daytime, but the Duchess is quite right: in the evening, it is fabulous.

The Banqueting Hall had been at the centre of castle life in medieval times. This dining room occupies the same site but is now slightly larger than it was then, measuring 60 feet by 24 feet/18 metres by 7.5 metres and 24 feet in height. When the 1st Duchess's Gothic interior was removed in the 1850s, the place where the dais stood in the medieval days could be seen at the southern end of the room. Over it was the buffet for the display of crystal cups, silver flagons and plate, with a lion's paw as the termination of a hood-mould, and on one side a small water-drain. The hooks for suspending the tapestry on the walls still remained in the old plaster. The alcove remains, and was used for breakfasting. It was here also that the 1st Duke and Duchess entertained the gentry on 'open days'.

The armorial wood ceiling is carved in Brunswick pine by the Alnwick School and decorated with the heraldry of the many baronies belonging to the house of Percy. The overall ceiling design concept is taken from the Basilica of San Lorenzo in Rome, although the Italian version is painted and gilded. The ceiling should be lighter in tone but someone cleaned it with linseed oil in the late 1950s, which darkened it.

The Duchess has installed ceiling lighting. Originally there were two gas lamps to light the room. You cannot see these, as they are above the ceiling and were wound down through two trap doors over the dining table. The Duke admits he has never dropped them down, but says, 'One day I would love to do it; I would love to restore them. I have been in there to have a look and all the machinery, the cranking handles, are there.'

Special vents allowed the stink of gas to escape upwards. The 4th Duke's very young wife, Duchess Eleanor, insisted that whatever colour dress she wore was matched by the colour of the light shades. As she was daughter of the 2nd Marquess of Westminster, the Grosvenor symbols are with the Percys' on the marble chimneypiece. The shiny silver restored fire surround is made mostly of high carbon steel, adorned with a copper alloy.

I saw this hearth being restored by two experts. Such restoration takes days of work and is an amazingly fiddly job, using many specialist liquids. At first glance, the hearth seemed

OPPOSITE Inspired by the gilded and painted ceiling of the Basilica of San Lorenzo in Rome, the armorial ceiling was carved in Brunswick pine by the Alnwick School of Carving, set up by the 4th Duke for his restoration. It should be lighter in tone but it was cleaned with linseed oil in the 1950s.
ABOVE The chimneypiece's classical symbols honour Dionysus. The male figure on the right is by Nucci, c.1825, of a mischievous bearded satyr, or faun, with the Roman god of wine Bacchus (in Greek called Dionysus) as a child holding the satyr's calve. The female figure with a goat, carved by Strazza, is of Bacchante, the mythological female follower of Bacchus. These creatures, with their crowns of ivy and vines, suggest passion, appetite and fertility, perhaps a curious choice by the childless 4th Duke and Duchess, whose Percy and Grosvenor symbols form the central carved coat of arms.

LEFT TO RIGHT One of a pair of George III silver-gilt dessert stands, from Paul Storr, London, *c.*1810, made for the 3rd Duke; Minton busts, made of Parian white marble, of the Duke of Wellington and Lord Nelson, on either side of a clock by Mangeant Monginot, Paris, 1750; the silver-gilt vase presented to Alan Ian Percy (later the 8th Duke) by the people of Alnwick when he married Helen in 1911.

fine. But as one of the experts showed me its problems, I realized how thorough the Duchess's conservation programme has been. The expert pointed out dots of rust all over the place, along with soot, dirt and debris. Green oxide had covered the copper alloy castings and every crevice was packed with hard old polish, which causes corrosion over time.

To the left of the fireplace is a rather good 1760 Japanese lacquered cabinet sitting on a Chinese Chippendale-style japanned stand. On the right is a Chinese Coromandel lacquered cabinet from 1800.

The lumpy but practical buffets were made locally in 1860. The dining chairs are mostly eighteenth century, but the dining table is Victorian, made of mahogany. It seats up to forty. The gold-looking silver-gilt candelabra and cups on the table are part of a huge set made for the 3rd Duke when he went to Paris for the coronation of Charles X. He was a Percy with a particular sense of the grand. At one end of the room you can see two Minton busts: one of the Duke of Wellington, the other of Lord Nelson. They are made of Parian white marble from Paros in Greece.

The walking sticks on display were made by Norman Tulip, a tenant on the estate who died in 1996. Made of rams' horns and bent to shape using heat, each takes hundreds of hours to make. 'The great tradition up here is stick picking among the farming community,' the Duke explains. 'The most famous stick dresser in the UK made these. He never sold one, but would sometimes give one or two away – he was the greatest. When he died, his family asked if we would take them on permanent loan. They are fantastic and the public home in on them – they are so different.' They are so beautifully made

that, if you look at the heron for example, you can almost feel the feathers on it. The royal family apparently have some too.

The Duchess had this room conserved and restored in 2006. The ceiling was cleaned and then waxed. The woodwork on the dados was polished, the walls re-silked in her green and a new carpet made. As in the Saloon and Drawing Room, the enormous carpet was designed by D. & S. Bamford and hand-made in Bulgaria. In addition, all the paintings were cleaned.

The dining room is dominated by paintings of the 1st Duke and Duchess in their coronation robes over the fireplace by Francis Lindo (late 1760s). However, the theme of most of the family portraits here is the nineteenth-century Percys. On the southern wall hangs a portrait of the 4th Duke by Sir Francis Grant (1857). The 5th Duke's portrait by Gustav Pope (1866) hangs on the north wall.

There is no room more devoted to the Percy lineage than this one. Hung here is an exhausting list of Earls and Dukes and their wives. All the important relatives are here.

Of the portrait of poor Thomas, 7th Earl, who died in 1572, by Phillips (1831), the Duke says, 'I bought the death warrant for this chap the other day. He was executed by Queen Elizabeth I for the rebellion of the Northern Isles. His death warrant came up in Christie's and I managed to buy it.'

OPPOSITE After the Library, this is the Duchess's favourite state room, in her view 'at its best when it is buzzing and full of people'. The table seats forty.
ABOVE LEFT One of the two lacquered cabinets on either side of the chimneypiece, a Chinese Coromandel cabinet from 1800.
ABOVE RIGHT Pavilions on an eighteenth-century Chinese lacquered screen.

THE BREAKFAST ROOM

During the winter months when the family live in the castle, this room is used by staff when there is a big dinner going on next door in the State Dining Room.

The 1st Duchess, using Robert Adam, redid this room in the 1760s. She and the 1st Duke would have breakfast here. Their bedrooms were above. Remarkably, it was untouched by the mid-nineteenth-century restoration but unfortunately the 6th Duke did not restore it when the Gothic hammerbeam

LEFT Dressed sticks and shepherd's crooks made by Norman Tulip. A George Snaith taught him how to make them, on condition that he never sold one.
ABOVE In the Octagonal Towers, what once was a wonderful Robert Adam Breakfast Room was sadly renovated by the 6th Duke in late Victorian 'Queen Anne' style. It is now used for exhibitions.

roof needed repair. He had it knocked down and employed the architect Eustace Balfour to restore the room in the 'Queen Anne' style.

The flat stucco ceiling is decorated with the heraldic design of a crescent and fetterlock. The walls are covered in old heavily embossed paper imitating leather which came from furnished rooms at Warkworth Castle, which the Percys once used. The fireplace surround is of Frosterly marble, a fossilized black limestone from County Durham.

The eighteenth-century painted canvas, which hangs above the gallery, is part of a set by the French artist Clermont. It used to decorate the marquees at Syon House when the 1st Duchess Elizabeth held her fabulous fêtes there in the eighteenth century.

The pair of paintings high up on either side of the fireplace, showing the castles of Alnwick and Warkworth, are by Peter Hartover (1670s/80s). The Alnwick painting provides a good picture of the castle before its eighteenth-century restoration. It also provides a view of the town of Alnwick.

The windows to this room are closed tight, as it is now used for exhibitions when the castle is open to the public.

THE CHINA GALLERY

"The new china gallery is Jane's idea,' says the Duke proudly. 'She wanted to show all this amazing china, most of which wasn't on display, or was at Syon just gathering dust. The Meissen was on display next door but not particularly well. When I was a child this was a picture gallery with some pretty ghastly family portraits and not much else.'

Salvin designed this to be a service passage. He told a session of the RIBA in 1856, 'I constructed a Passage across the Gateway, and at the end a Lift from the Kitchen, by which the patties may travel in safety.' This passage links up to a jib door into the Upper Guard Chamber and passes alongside the State Dining Room, Drawing Room and Saloon. When the Duke and Duchess took on the castle in 1995, it was a 'nasty' green colour, enhanced by fluorescent strip lighting.

The Duchess employed the Curator of Porcelain at Waddesdon Manor, Selma Schwartz, to design the corridor as a 'porcelain room'. The concept of 'upholstering' a room's wall from top to toe in china, as seen here, derives from the German courts in the first half of the eighteenth century. The most famous example ever created was the extraordinary Japanese Palace in Dresden by the 'King of Meissen', Augustus the Strong, Elector of Saxony and King of Poland, who started

the Meissen factory, the first in Europe to succeed in making hard-paste porcelain of the Chinese type.

The wall is made up of Meissen, Paris and Chelsea porcelain. Selma Schwartz explains that the gallery was made 'by creating a dado above which there would be "panels" divided by pilasters running up to the cornice. Decorative designs, made by the porcelain in each panel, would resemble carved designs on wooden panelling. The large number of Paris plates meant that they could be used as the "columns" . . . unifying the whole scheme.' A succession of new mirrors placed opposite the windows not only increases the natural light but establishes a rhythm down the length of the gallery. Planning where each piece went must have been a nightmare.

There are two eighteenth-century Meissen services here. The first is the Hanbury Williams Service, made in the late 1740s. It is a dinner service with incredible animals, foliage and insects, and it includes some of the earliest pieces of hard-paste porcelain made in Europe. It was given to Charles Hanbury Williams, who was British envoy to the Saxon court in Dresden. Hanbury sent it to Holland House, in London's Holland Park – the home of Lord and Lady Holland. No one is quite sure how the Northumberlands acquired it, but it is likely that the 1st Duchess did. Whatever the case, in September 1940, Nazi bombs devastated most of Holland House, so in a sense the Northumberlands saved these German plates.

The 'guide for the guides' describes the Hanbury service. 'The theme of the decoration is swags of flowers surrounding, mainly, hunting scenes based on etchings by Reidinger. Other animals were inspired by, or copied from, early sixteenth century Dürer wood cuts of exotic animals. The soup tureens and covers were modelled by Joachim Kaendler, Meissen's master sculptor. The insects, used to cover flaws, have been traced to engravings from a book dated 1592 by Jakob Hoefinagel. The soup plates are decorated with pictures of birds taken from a set of colour engravings by Eleaser Albin's *A Natural History of Birds of Britain* published 1731–8. It has been suggested that it was intended as a "hunting service" as no other Meissen service has so many *glochen* (covers). These *glochen* covered a flat, double metal plate of either pewter or silver that held hot water in an attempt to keep food hot.'

RIGHT Since 1995, the Duchess has gone to great lengths to use everything in storage, and no room illustrates this more than here. On show, together for the first time, are the two Meissen services, one Paris service and some Chelsea porcelain in what was hitherto the old Picture Gallery. Salvin designed it as a service corridor.

The second Meissen service, called the Marcolini Service, was made in the 1780s and named after the man who ran the German porcelain factory. It is a rare collection, decorated with scenes from Aesop's fables. Each piece of porcelain here is individually hand painted with scenes from the fables, such as 'The Fox and the Grapes', 'The Tortoise and the Hare' and 'The Boy Who Cried', and the title of each is written on the back. The Meissen factory copied illustrations by Oudry in an eighteenth-century edition of Aesop's fables by La Fontaine, which Waddesdon Manor has in its library. The Duchess had these etchings copied, framed and hung as near to the appropriate plate as possible.

The China Gallery also displays the gilded Paris Dagoty Dessert Service, bought by the 3rd Duke when he was Ambassador in Paris in 1825. Honori Dagoty made china for Bonaparte's extravagant wife, Empress Josephine. The service is decorated with scenes of France, Italy and Switzerland.

The castle's Triangle collection of Chelsea porcelain includes one of Sprimont's famous Goat and Bee jugs. A former silversmith, Nicholas Sprimont, started making Chelsea porcelain in London. Most of his early wares were quite figurative, often in plain white, influenced by his silver design, and bore an incised triangle mark.

The gallery has some plates and dishes of Red Anchor ware made in the Chelsea porcelain factory in the 1750s. These have fruit and leaves in relief or strawberry borders. If Red Anchor was inspired by Meissen, the next phase of the Chelsea factory in the 1760s was more influenced by Sèvres and is called Gold Anchor ware. It is heavily gilded and very colourful, often painted yellow, blue, green and red. Here there are part of a Gold Anchor dessert service painted with birds and some vases.

The China Gallery also houses some brightly painted sixteenth-century Limoges enamels, based on 1502 illustrations of Virgil's *Opera*. Experts believe that these once decorated the panelling of Catherine de' Medici's Cabinet des Amours. Duchess Helen, the Duke's grandmother, had them in her boudoir, now the Manuscript Room.

LEFT The Duchess worked with Selma Schwartz to show the Percy porcelain, basing the display on the early eighteenth-century idea of porcelain rooms, which came to the fore in German courts, the most famous being the Japanese Palace in Dresden. Clever mirrors add light, and help establish a rhythm the length of the gallery.

THE CHAPEL

If you walk up the Grand Staircase and turn right and right again, you come to the gallery of the Chapel. The Chapel was added to the Keep by Salvin. With its Gothic ceiling and lancet windows, it looks like an English Victorian church.

Up to the Victorian and Edwardian era, every servant had to attend prayers daily at eight in the morning in the pews of the Chapel; the family sat in the gallery. The family now prefer to attend St Michael's Church in Alnwick town, which is only five minutes' walk away, and was where Lady Catherine Percy was married in 2011.

There used to be a chapel in the Inner Bailey, close to the Constable's Tower. You can see part of the roof in Canaletto's painting of the castle, now hung in the Saloon and shown on page 22. The 1st Duke and Duchess knocked down this chapel, and in fact many scattered buildings within the walls of the castle, during the restoration of the eighteenth century.

The Robert Adam chapel they built in the new castle wing from the Keep to the Middle Gateway has since been knocked down too. It gave way to Salvin's suite of private rooms for the 4th Duke, Algernon, and his wife, Duchess Eleanor. The only remains of Adam's chapel are the Gothic lectern and priest's chair near the altar here.

The beautiful tapestries here were purchased in Europe by the 4th Duke on his Grand Tours for Warkworth Castle. The 10th Duke put them up in the 1960s and in doing so hid the walls' Italian designs in marble mosaic.

The two biggest tapestries depict the baptism and vision of the first Christian Roman emperor, Constantine the Great, who founded Constantinople as the capital of the eastern Roman Empire. The tapestries were made in Paris in the early seventeenth century. The three smaller Aubusson tapestries show the Old Testament story of Tobias, who finds a cure for his father's blindness. The Chapel also houses *The Nativity*, painted in 1605 by Giovanno Lanfranco.

As you can see, there are many flags here. The oldest dates from 1780 and is the King's Colour and Regimental Colour of the Northumberland Militia. This flag was carried to London during the battle against the Gordon Riots. The government used about 11,000 troops to quell an orgy of anti-Catholic looting and street violence. Three hundred or so rioters died. Other flags include banners of the Percy Tenantry Volunteers and a King's Colour and Regimental Colour of the Northumberland Militia – all dating from the start of the nineteenth century. The most recent flag is the Regimental Standards of the Northumberland Fusiliers from the 1950s.

LEFT Designed by Salvin, the Chapel has a three-light apse. The lower walls have fine medieval-style mosaic decorations with compartments of Alexandrine work, like those in ancient basilicas, but now are covered with French tapestries that came from Warkworth Castle. The three by the altar are 1750s Aubussons; the detail (below left) of one made in Paris in 1625 shows the baptism of the first Christian emperor, Constantine the Great. BELOW RIGHT The priest's chair is a fine and rare example of Robert Adam's late Gothic style.

THE PRIVATE ROOMS

ITHIN THE KEEP are eight state rooms, forty-eight family and guest rooms, and seventeen household rooms. There are no private or public rooms per se. The family live here for half the year without a rope, tourist sign or guide in sight. However, if you look at Robert Adam's plans of the eighteenth century and Anthony Salvin's and Luigi Canina's of the next century, you will see that the castle always had smaller, cosier rooms for the family, the state rooms being used for grander guest occasions. Here we take a peek at all the family rooms not included in the summer official tour. Rooms occupied by the household and Collections and Archives Department are in the next chapter.

Some of the guest bedrooms are along the Warkworth Corridor, which faces northwards looking to the River Aln, on the second floor and above the state rooms. Others are along the Lovaine Corridor, also on the second floor, which is above the Duke and Duchess's studies and private dining room on the Boudoir Corridor, which faces south-west towards the Barbican, Gatehouse and Clock Tower. On the third floor above the Lovaine Corridor is another guestroom corridor called the Hotspur Corridor. If the two spare bedrooms in the family's Prudhoe Tower are added to the bedrooms in the Warkworth, Lovaine and Hotspur Corridors, there are about thirteen bedrooms for guests. With the family ones, you can count eighteen bedrooms altogether.

THE PRIVATE ENTRANCE

For such an outdoor family (while I was photographing the rooms, if the Duke was setting out to take the dogs for a walk and passed me, typically he would say, 'Oh, still here. Are you not going outside?'), it is appropriate to start with the wellies. At the bottom of the Grand Staircase off the Lower Guard Chamber, through glass-framed doors, is the family entrance. Until the Duke and Duchess moved in after 1995 this room and indeed the whole of the lower ground floor was used as planned by Salvin for staff.

LEFT From the family's entrance this corridor leads to the new private kitchen created by the Duchess. Charles Hesp painted the faux stone to match the existing stone that was found under the plaster.

ABOVE The Duke and Duchess in the Inner Courtyard, before taking the dogs for a walk in Hulne Park in 2007.

The Duke and Duchess and children leave their boots here, hanging up an Armada-sized number of coats, waxed jackets, hats, caps and so on. Some of the Duchess's hats are in the wicker baskets and one or two on the busts. In the alcove windows is a pair of Laurence Macdonald marble busts of the 4th Duke, Algernon, and Duchess Eleanor, souvenirs from their 1853–4 Rome trip.

FAMILY KITCHEN

Passing the two loos, once staff loos and now for everyone, you leave the Private Entrance, turn right and walk along a corridor to the Family Kitchen, which sits directly underneath the Library at the base of the Prudhoe Tower. The word 'kitchen' is a misnomer here: the main room is a casual family dining room with a kitchen at one end. Off one side through an arch is a cosy sitting room with a television, matched on the other side by a billiard room.

The kitchen is the Duchess's favourite room. 'Aside from our bedrooms, I wanted to have one room in the castle,

ABOVE These busts by Laurence Macdonald are of the 4th Duke and Duchess, made in Rome during their 1853–4 trip to Paris, Frankfurt, Switzerland, Milan, Florence, Rome and Naples which had such a major impact on what we see today in the castle in terms of artwork and the design of the state rooms.

OPPOSITE The small L-shaped private entrance for the family used to be a staff area but now has many useful pegs for a plethora of outdoor clothes and (below) two useful loos.

preferably a big kitchen, where the children always knew that they would find me and where we congregated. Finding me was going to be difficult, because obviously the castle is so big. We made this fantastic kitchen and this is the heart of the house for us.'

In doing this the Duchess was effectively breaking up the castle's Victorian 'upstairs/downstairs' layout. Until Duke Harry's time this area had housed the housekeeper's room, a room for mending furniture and next door to that a staff kitchen. 'With new arches, we turned these staff rooms into one big room, and by taking off the plaster we found this original stonework.'

Charles Hesp painted around the new arches to match the stonework. The furniture was all hand-made on the estate from oak. Bar stools near the Aga are a good spot to use the Wi-Fi and tip-tap away. By themselves or with only a few guests, the family have breakfast and most meals here. For breakfast sausages, bacon, fried eggs, tomatoes and mushrooms, as well as porridge, are cooked daily in the cook's kitchen and kept warm on the Aga here.

In the sitting-room area, a new fireplace was made in 1998 with local stone. The family watch movies on TV here. Through the other arch is a billiard table that at one time sat in the front hall. The zebra head on the wall over the entrance originates from the 1930s, when the Duke's uncle, the 9th

Duke, who was killed in 1940, went to Africa on shoots.

When the Duchess moved into the castle, her four children – George, Catherine, Melissa and Max – were very young. 'I wanted a normal life for them. I hated the idea of them growing up not being able to do anything for themselves. So, although the cook has her own kitchen down the corridor, it was important that we had our own Aga somewhere. I think the Aga is the heart of any old family house in the country – it is really important.'

I am quite sure the Duchess has not cooked on hers, but the family might. 'If the children wanted to sleep in until eleven o'clock in the morning they could, but they would have to cook their own breakfast. Until we arrived, the castle kitchen was just for the cook. But in our new room they have got whatever they need, and put their things in the dishwasher. That was important to me too.' And I have seen the youngest daughter,

---

OPPOSITE More than a kitchen, this private area underneath the Library in the Prudhoe Tower is the new heart of the house for the family and central to the Duchess's innovations since 1995. She turned numerous staff rooms into one T-shaped space by creating arches, and by removing 1850s plasterwork exposed the castle's stonework.

BELOW The Duchess thought it was very important that as a family they had their own Aga, seen here on the left.

Melissa, dripping in icing, practise her cake-making here.

When the Duchess married, becoming Lady Percy, she and her husband lived in West Sussex for seven years before moving to Chatton Park, a Georgian house about 10 miles/ 16 kilometres north of the castle. The Duchess explains, 'Everybody in my generation started to live in their kitchen with a sofa in it so that whoever was cooking was talking to either their friends or their children at the same time. And that was what we had always had in all our married life. There was no reason not to have it here at Alnwick too.'

Ian August oversaw the kitchen conversion. 'None of these archways was here before. The new kitchen sits below the Library and the big question, when we started creating these openings, was what effect the weight that sits above was having. We have cellars underneath too. Other generations would never do this, but with Her Grace's new plan it brought their private accommodation down on to the staff level – so we all worked, so to speak, on one level.'

Such thinking brought advantages. 'If they want the staff to have the night off,' says Ian August, 'they can simply walk along the corridor and just trolley things along themselves. You lose that age-old upstairs/downstairs issue. It means you have a much closer working relationship with your staff than you ever did in the past. This is one of the things that I admire about this Duchess. At one time, the family would know the housekeeper but they perhaps had no idea who the cleaning staff were below. I feel it has possibly become a family home more than it has ever been before.'

BOUDOIR CORRIDOR

Leaving the Family Kitchen you follow a passage to the foot of the private staircase, alongside the Chapel. On the landing of this staircase you pass a George II mahogany table, George III chairs and some wall mirrors. One of these is a George I giltwood mirror, topped with carved fruit grasped in the beak of an eagle, forming the crest; it came from Stanwick Park. On the pier tables is a nineteenth-century Canton dish and trays, and a Chinese *famille-verte* dish, Kangxi, painted with a phoenix flying overhead. There is a lift, but honouring the

adage 'Use it or lose it', most fly up the stairs to the Boudoir Corridor. This is off the Upper Guard Chamber on the first floor of the castle.

This has been a bedroom corridor since at least 1760. When the 1st Duchess restored the castle Robert Adam made here two big bedrooms, each with a dressing room. Salvin kept to the same plan in 1856. When Duchess Helen moved out of Alnwick in 1939 and the castle temporarily turned into a school, these rooms were used as dormitories. The name Boudoir Corridor originates from the Duke's parents' time, when in 1947 Duchess Elizabeth made the first big bedroom her boudoir. Today the Duke and Duchess each have a study here in two former dressing rooms, and there is one large dining room plus another large office for secretaries. During the week, the area is very much a place for work.

The colour of the corridor is cream with the architecture picked out in bold painted panelling in a soft red-pink colour. The colours were hand-mixed by the talented Charles Hesp.

Along the corridor is a Louis XVI carved giltwood bergère, c.1780, one of a set covered in strawberry-red silk upholstery. The chair has beautiful carved scrollwork of husks and flowers. The brass hexagonal lantern is William IV and, like many lanterns here, came from Northumberland House. The mahogany dining chair with its moulded cartouche-shaped back came from Syon House. Most dominant is the ornate oak and gilded bookcase designed by Montiroli.

Opposite Duchess Elizabeth's boudoir, which is now the Private Dining Room, *The Madonna of the Pinks*, attributed to Raphael, once hung. The painting arrived at Alnwick as part of the Camuccini Collection in 1854. The Duke's elder brother loaned it to the National Gallery for a decade or so. When the Getty Museum in Los Angeles offered to buy it, the National Gallery, led by Charles Saumarez Smith, launched a highly public campaign to keep it, which it eventually did in 2003, paying £22 million. Much of the proceeds went into a 'chattels fund' to conserve everything here.

It was a controversial time, with some art experts – forgetting the meaning of the word 'loan' – implying that the painting was the 'nation's heritage'. Others thought that the British gallery should not spend its entire acquisitions budget on one 'small shiny' Italian painting – especially when, although the National Gallery had verified its authenticity, the attribution to Raphael was causing division among experts. In the light of personal attacks on the Duke, fears were expressed in private that such criticism would reduce the willingness of others to lend in the future. Perhaps some of the criticism was inspired by jealously, nationalism or anti-Americanism. Supporters

LEFT The kitchen's cosy sitting room is where the Duke and Duchess and their children congregate most, when they are by themselves and want to watch the telly. Retrieved from storage by the Duchess, most of the animal heads originate from the 1930s safaris of the Duke's uncle, the 9th Duke.

In honour of the feminine concept of a boudoir, the Duchess has hung other paintings of women along this corridor. The first painting you see is of a Queen Anne lady in a voluptuous brown silk gown, painted by a follower of Peter Lely. Other paintings include two Umbrian early Italian Renaissance works after Pietro Perugino, *The Madonna and Child Enthroned with St Anne* (or *The family of St Anne*) and *Saint Mary of Egypt and Saint Catherine of Alexandria* – a pair framed as one and acquired with the Camuccini Collection.

One of the 1st Duchess paintings after Van Dyck of Diana Russell, Countess of Oxford (1630s), is here. In her journals the Duchess named it 'Head of the Countess of Morton'. The *prime version* is in Madrid's Prado.

Another painting is more tragic. It is a portrait of Miss Rosa Bathurst, dressed in white with a crimson trim. She was known to be extremely beautiful but died aged sixteen in 1824. She was engaged to Algernon Percy, a grandson of the 1st Duke and Duchess. When they were out riding together along the banks of the River Tiber in Rome her horse – which he had just given her – took fright. The horse slipped off the path down the banks into the raging river. Rosa screamed for help but was swept away and drowned. Their riding companion, Lady Aylmer, wrote that the river was 'so tremendously increased by the melted snows from the mountains, that no human aid could save her'. Algernon wore mourning clothes for two years, and while he became an ambassador in Berne, Switzerland, he never married. He died on a visit to London nine years after Rosa's death, from a violent three-hour attack of cholera.

of the Duke tended to come from the private sector, who understood that the Italian painting was purchased privately for a private home and could be sold as such; like anyone on the BBC's *Antiques Roadshow*, one likes to sell the odd heirloom to fund something else. Few critics appreciated the financial burden to the new Duke of having to deal with death duties after his brother's sudden demise, and having to maintain land and buildings on the Northumberland Estates (starting with 20 tonnes of new lead on the roof to prevent rot), not to mention paying for the much-needed conservation of hundreds and hundreds of art treasures at both Syon Park and Alnwick Castle.

Fortunately the Duke has broad shoulders and a sense of humour. When Sotheby's Henry Wyndham and I accompanied the Duke to the National Gallery to sign the contract and get his cheque for *The Madonna*, the beaming Charles Saumarez Smith offered pink champagne and, cheque in hand, the Duke asked to see his painting for one last time. Peering mischievously at it, he said drily, 'I wonder if it is, after all, a fake.'

ABOVE At the foot of the private staircase, on the principal level leading directly from the state rooms and seen here from the Boudoir Corridor, is the family entrance to the upper gallery of the Chapel.

RIGHT Looking down the Boudoir Corridor, which the Duchess had redecorated after 1995, the door to the right leads into her study. When the 1st Duchess restored the castle, Robert Adam made here two state bedrooms, each with a dressing room. Now sold, *The Madonna of the Pinks*, attributed to Raphael, c.1506–7, once hung on this family corridor.

PRIVATE DINING ROOM

Aside from the ceiling, this room has a Georgian theme. With its worn gold silk walls and the 1st Duke and Duchess's eighteenth-century Georgian furniture and paintings, the atmosphere is decidedly evocative of the *ancien régime*.

A Rocky Landscape by Jan Brueghel the Younger (mid-seventeenth century) is a wonderful example of the 1st Duchess's taste for the art of the Low Countries, and of seventeenth-century Flemish Baroque from Antwerp. It shows, in minute colourful detail, pilgrims resting and monks preparing food. If you look carefully, you will see that there is a priest celebrating mass in a grotto.

A second Brueghel, from the Camuccini Collection, is by Jan Brueghel the Elder, painted on copper. *The Garden of Eden* (1616) depicts Adam and Eve and a lion and lioness, a giraffe, camel, horse, tigers and oxen. There is a larger version of the same composition in the Galleria Doria Pamphili in Rome. A third painting to the right of the chimneypiece is the seventeenth-century *A Concert Champêtre with Many Figures before a Town*, by a follower of David Vinckeboons.

Two other treats here are the large north and south views of *Bay of Naples* in 1742 by Claude Joseph Vernet. The 1st Duchess might have liked these, for they show ordinary people messing about on the shore, but I was surprised to hear that they were purchased in 1961, by the Duke's father, Duke Hugh. He was not known to like spending pennies on anything inside, but he was in fact quite a connoisseur of the arts, as these astute acquisitions reveal.

The *ancien régime* continues with Charles Philips's 1732 ensemble of Algernon, 7th Duke of Somerset, at a dice board, near his wife, their daughter Lady Elizabeth Seymour (the future 1st Duchess) and other figures. The 1st Duchess's brother, Lord Beauchamp, is in the scene as a child in long clothes, holding his mother's hand. Had he not died young, the Percys might forever have been called Somerset, and the Northumberland duchy would not have been reborn.

Another informal scene is in the painting of Elizabeth's husband, Hugh, as 1st Duke, by Johann Zoffany (1760s). Being given some deeds, the Duke is seated in a pink coat and

---

RIGHT AND PAGES 116–7 The side tables are 1750s George II, and came from Stanwick Park. By the door, the gilt, *breche-violette* marble-top console table with a Chinese fret frieze is particularly good. Above the Nucci chimneypiece is a beautiful George III giltwood pier mirror that belonged to the 1st Duchess. The chandelier is George III, *c.*1790.

breeches with a gold vest and, of course, wearing with pride his Garter ribbon. The interior shown is the Tapestry Room at Northumberland House with its amazing Soho textiles.

It's all George here. The two side tables are 1750s George II, from Stanwick Park. The parcel-gilt, *breche violette* marble-top side tables with their Chinese fret friezes are particularly lovely and came from Stanwick Park. The George III card tabled belonged to the 1st Duchess, Elizabeth Seymour, and were made of satinwood and marquetry by John Linnell in the 1770s. Above the Nucci marble chimneypiece is a beautiful George III giltwood pier mirror that also belonged to her. The chandelier, one of the best in the castle, is also George III, *c*.1790, as is the bowed mahogany sideboard.

LEFT Two details from *Bay of Naples from the South*, 1742, by Claude Joseph Vernet, which the 10th Duke acquired in 1961. Also hung here is his *Bay of Naples from the North*. Both are typical of the *veduta esatta* (Italian for exact view) style of this French seascape artist.

ABOVE A detail of *A Rocky Landscape*, by Jan Brueghel the Younger, mid-seventeenth century, a delightful example of the 1st Duchess's taste for Flemish Baroque, showing pilgrims praying and monks preparing food.

The mahogany dining table is George IV but has one odd embellishment. When the table is set for dinner the Duke has some silver pieces at his end and the Duchess has hers: 'My children bought me a silver dung beetle from Patrick Mavros in London. On holiday in Africa I was fascinated by these busy beetles and am very fond of my silver one.'

When the house is full of guests, during the shooting season, breakfast is served here. Ladies can have breakfast in bed. It is also used for lunch and dinner.

The ceiling had become lost under layers of cigar smoke, according to Ian August, so 'we put a scaffold up and found the original colours, got them remade and then redecorated.'

Sadly the silk walls are on their last legs. 'The rooms here need re-silking,' says the Duchess. Mindful of the next heirs, she says, 'George wanted to do it green again. He loves the green of the State Dining Room. I don't know, because we have breakfast here and the green is fine at night but not so good in the day. But, whatever I do now, I will always ask George. He is the one who is going to have to live with it. And he is very like me: he likes light, which you don't get much of in this place.' I wonder if George will choose something Georgian.

THE DUCHESS'S STUDY

Next door, in what used to be a dressing room, is the Duchess's refuge. 'I love my study because it is my little haven.' Lined with old gold silk walls, the room is snug, and always scented with candles. Books and papers are piled on the ottoman, which is next to a small cushion-strewn sofa and an upholstered armchair.

Among the piles of paper on top of the ottoman I spotted a private manual for new Lord Lieutenants – a sort of 'how to do it'. Lord Lieutenants are the representatives of the Crown for each county and the Duchess was appointed Lord Lieutenant of Northumberland in 2009 by the Queen, on the advice of the Prime Minister. There is also a book called *All-Round Genius: The Unknown Story of Britain's Greatest Sportsman* about Max Woosnam, the Duchess's great-uncle, 'my amazing ancestor'. Among his many talents, he was captain of the English football team and a 1920 Olympic tennis gold medallist. 'I think my children get their sporty side from him, as much as the Percys.'

In the alcove by the window, on a small oval table, is the Duchess's laptop. A fire is lit most of the time in winter. Above the chimneypiece is a William IV carved giltwood mirror. On the chimneypiece are photographs of the Duchess's children and a dog, plus a stuffed rat. 'I prefer the rats to look as though they are running,' the Duchess explains with a twinkle in her eye. 'I sometimes take rats as presents instead of chocolates or a book. We always have rats outside around us in Scotland and people now give me things too. The other day I was handed three white stoats, which are in the freezer.'

The Duchess now owns about twenty stuffed dogs. 'I have always loved things which are different,' she says. 'I love dogs as pets and when they die, I never see that it is any worse having a dog that you have loved stuffed and sitting on the floor. However, my family are not so keen, so I don't have our dogs stuffed. Instead, I collect stuffed dogs from a great taxidermist in Europe. He has a licence to get dogs when they are being put down and he calls me when he thinks one might be of interest. I like them looking as though this is their home, so they sit around in chairs or lie by the fires in the guest bedrooms. I really love them and I move them around wherever I go – they are my most treasured possessions.'

There are a few paintings in the study. One is by Caroline Stanhope of Rubens's wife (1838), but it is not known if it is Isabella Brant or Rubens' second wife, Hélène Fourment. The second is a pretty late eighteenth-century portrait by Hoppner of Charlotte Percy, afterwards Countess of Ashburnham.

Hoppner did a series of 'ladies of rank and fashion'. The father of Charlotte was the 1st Earl of Beverley and the second son of the 1st Duke and Duchess, and the present Duke is the direct descendant of this Beverley line, by the 5th Duke. Sixth Duchess Louisa's mother, Anne Drummond, is here too.

There is also an eighteenth-century painting by Joshua Reynolds of Charles, 2nd Marquess of Rockingham, twice a prime minister and here wearing his peer's robes.

ABOVE The Duchess is an avid collector of taxidermy – mostly of dogs but, showing her quirky side, even of stuffed rats. On the chimneypiece in her study are photographs of her children, including this cut-out of Lord Max Percy, her younger son, in his school clothes.

RIGHT From the 1750s this was a dressing room, but it is now Duchess's study and sanctuary. She gave most of the interviews for this book here, by the fire.

presents being wrapped up – in June. Work relating to her many charitable interests takes place and on her *The Poison Diaries* trilogy. Her duties as Duchess on the estate are organized from here too, including staff functions and the castle's annual Christmas party for children connected to the estate.

Every day is different for the Duchess. 'I might have meetings over at the gardens, or have a day doing Lord Lieutenancy work. In 2010 and 2011 we had many parades for soldiers returning from Afghanistan – I try to go to as many of these types of event as possible. My husband and I like to support lots of charities in the region, so that can keep us busy.' The Duchess's diary secretary says she is often booked six months in advance, and even more when there is a royal visit to the county.

THE DUKE'S STUDY

The Duke uses the same study that his father used. As in the Duchess's Study, the silk walls, here in red, have a charming fray to them. Some say the silk was copied from Northumberland House.

The room is a man's room, with dog cushions strewn across the floor for the Duke's cocker spaniels, maps and prints leaning against this and that, piles of books and hunting apparel and photos of his children and wife scattered around the room. The Duke's mahogany desk by the window looking out over the Outer Bailey dominates. It dates from 1775 and came from Northumberland House. No scented candles on this one.

The Duke is not an equestrian but has five chargers on his walls, painted by James Ward in the 1820s. 'These have always been here,' the Duke says, pointing out each horse. One is Nonpareil, the favourite dark bay charger of the Prince Regent. There is the white charger of George III on a hill and Count Platoff's white charger next to five of his Cossacks. The most famous horse here is Copenhagen, Wellington's favourite. It was commissioned by Hugh, the 3rd Duke, for 100 guineas. And there is Marengo, the white Arab charger ridden by Napoleon Bonaparte at the Battle of Waterloo. 'And that is my father's Munnings,' says the Duke, pointing to a charming racing scene of racehorses in the paddock at Epsom in the 1930s. Alfred Munnings lost the sight from one eye in an accident when he was twenty yet is a much admired British early twentieth-century horse artist.

The last 'charger' painting in here is of Margaret Renwick, the indomitable housekeeper at Alnwick from 1912 to 1948.

THE DUKE AND DUCHESS'S SECRETARIES' OFFICE

Further along the corridor before the Duke's Study you come to the office for the Duke and Duchess's two secretaries. Until recently, they had only one secretary, but the workload has steadily increased over the years. Before 1995, this large red room used to be the dining room. Under both Salvin's and Adam's plans, it was an important bedroom.

This room is now an important office, the place of much hard work supporting the Duchess, and indeed the Duke, professionally and domestically. Everything is planned months ahead. Once, I was astonished to see hundreds of Christmas

LEFT This room was designed as a state bedroom in the 1850s and the Duke's parents used it as their dining room, but it is now the office of the Duke and Duchess's secretaries.

ABOVE The Duchess at work (right). Though she is married into an old family, she is a modern woman and not a slave to the past. She eschews the title 'chatelaine', saying that being Duchess is simply a job, and aside from running the Alnwick Garden and the house, she is a patron or president of eighty charities and organizations.

Mrs Renwick had served Duchess Helen and when her daughter-in-law, now the Dowager Duchess Elizabeth, became the mistress of the house in 1947 Mrs Renwick remained very much in charge. 'She had been there forever and she did things her way. I just followed along, doing what I was told, pretty much. These old people do keep things going,' the Dowager Duchess says. Sir Oswald Birley painted Mrs Renwick while staying at Alnwick Castle in 1948 for the Dowager Duchess's husband, the 10th Duke. Mrs Renwick would surely have been proud to remain in the Duke's study.

The Duke not only is passionate about nature conservation but will, I suspect, go down in the castle's history as the 'Conservation Duke'. Reflecting his interest in caring for the collection, there is a mass of art auction catalogues in the study. Although the art collection holds a few twentieth-century paintings, for instance by Munnings, Birley and de László, there is nothing more contemporary at Alnwick. 'We are happy to conserve,' the Duke says. 'I have commissioned a lot of watercolours, particularly landscapes, but these are

mainly at Burncastle. Nothing that would fit into the collection here.' The Duke values and enjoys working with his three full-time Collections and Archives staff at the castle, who, among other duties, help him monitor the art market. 'What is fun is buying things like Elizabeth I's death warrant for an ancestor, with her signature on it. And the other day I bought some more porcelain for gaps in the China Gallery. When things like that come up we snap them up.'

BELOW The Duke's Study is a couple of doors down from his wife's on the Boudoir Corridor and, like hers, was designed as a dressing room, but used to be his father's study. Neither has been restored. The Duke's two springer spaniels keep him company here.

RIGHT On his study walls the Duke has five paintings of chargers, painted by James Ward.

THE PRIVATE STAIRCASE

The origins of the second and third floors go back at least to the eighteenth century, when the 1st Duchess transformed the castle. The shell of what we see now along and off all the corridors on these floors is Anthony Salvin's 1850s transformation, but while some of the architectural detail might be Victorian, all the bedrooms have since 1995 been renovated by the current Duchess.

The style is vaguely late twentieth-century English country house, sympathetic to the existing structure but not replicating the 1850s. Nor is there much sign of the Italianate style found in the state rooms. The furniture, china and art are predominantly Georgian and Victorian, with a good dollop of Louis.

In the private side today the walls and carpet may be new but, aside from colour and fabrics, the English country house style here relies heavily on furniture that already existed – the contents of former Percy homes – as the Duchess's aim is to use everything that was hitherto in storage, restore it and reupholster it. The mixing of styles that results is partly because in the entire private side there are now roughly sixty pieces of Victorian furniture, seventy Georgian, forty Louis XV and a sprinkling of William IV, William and Mary, and Queen Anne.

Both Colefax and Fowler and Robert Kime have helped here and there, but it was Lucy Manners who helped the most with the interior design. Lucy's father had known the Dowager Duchess Elizabeth, but Lucy admits, 'It was a nice surprise to get a call. After a few trips to the castle, I was able to do it from a distance. Patrick Garner, the butler, was my go-between with the Duchess and it worked really well. She is very decisive, which is a great way to work. And Patrick was highly efficient and very good with the children.'

Their work was largely confined to putting together ideas for each bedroom and supplying storyboards with swatches of fabric and trim, from which the Duchess could make her selection. From this Charles Hesp worked with the Duchess on choosing wall and paint finishes. The household controller, Patrick Garner, worked extensively with the Duchess in many areas, from sourcing bed linen and finding new rugs to working with the London curtain-maker and upholsterer Thomson-Shultz Ltd. As crucial was the high standard of the work of the painters and joiners from the estate's Clerk of Works department. They continue to be essential for ongoing maintenance and conservation. While the Duchess is fond of blue and white flowers, inside the castle she prefers warm colours. The staircase walls are painted in a burnt-orange

wash to contrast with a raspberry-scarlet carpet designed by Wilton with a foliate design in sage and beige. Subtlety was key, as Robin Smeaton explains. 'The colours were specifically chosen not to be too bright. Her Grace was very conscious that she didn't want the carpet to jump out and be too strong, so softer tones have been used.' Indeed, all the new carpets are particularly well thought out, especially the Wilton ones.

On the semi-landing between the first and second floors Salvin's Victorian take on the medieval contrasts with Georgian giltwood furniture, a pair of George III semi-elliptical pier tables with an urn on each stretcher. These used to be at 17 Prince's Gate in London, once a London home to the Percy family. On the tables are some multicoloured Chinese nineteenth-century Cantonese porcelain and Kangxi dishes.

Above one table is a John Vardy-styled George I carved giltwood mirror that came from Stanwick Park. Hung above another table is a graceful painting by Sir Francis Grant in 1861 of Lady Mary Craven holding a black-and-red-feathered hat; daughter of Admiral Charles Philip Yorke, 4th Earl of Hardwicke, she married William George Craven. These are ancestors of the Duke's grandmother, Duchess Helen. The National Gallery has some early, less flattering photographs of Lady Mary in the Camille Silvy collection.

ABOVE Both the Duke's parents and grandparents loved fox hunting. His father acquired this painting in 1949, *Ralph John Lambton on his Hunter* by James Ward, 1820. The hounds are finely done. A number of related paintings hang on the walls of the Private Staircase and on the landings
RIGHT The painting on the wall is *Lady Mary Craven*, by Sir Francis Grant, 1861. Lady Mary Craven was the daughter of Admiral Charles Philip Yorke, 4th Earl of Hardwicke, both ancestors of the 8th Duchess, Helen.

LEFT TO RIGHT The private staircase leads up to the Prudhoe Tower, where the family bedrooms are; on the first semi-landing is a pair of George III semi-elliptical pier tables; the view out of the Upper Guard Chamber, showing the staircase walls painted by Charles Hesp to contrast with a new carpet designed by Wilton.

There are a painting of Warkworth Castle and some 1930s hunt scenes acquired by the 10th Duke by Lionel Edwards of the Percy Hunt at Kimmer Loch and at the Vale of Whittingham; also one of the 8th Duke hunting and another of his wife, Duchess Helen, out riding with two of her children.

On other walls here, a more republican theme is carried by suits of armour and swords left at Alnwick by Cromwell's forces after the Battle of Dunbar. 'Every single piece has at least one dent,' says the Duke.

The view up the thick carpeted steps to the second-floor landing is of George II gold furniture, with a 1750s carved giltwood console table, Siena marble top and double-scrolled cabriole legs beneath a 1745 gilded mirror. Next to the table is a Louis XV chair with cabriole legs.

Before you go up to the Prudhoe Tower you see a large oil painting by James Ward, *Ralph John Lambton on his Hunter* (1820), purchased in 1949 by the Duke's father, the 10th Duke. 'That is a great painting of Ralph Lambton and his sporting hounds,' the Duke says. 'It really is a very spectacular painting because every single hound is different – each rib shows.'

THE PRUDHOE TOWER

'The Prudhoe Tower is much to be admired, and no one seeing Alnwick Castle since its erection could suppose it was an addition to the old building. Duke Algernon (the fourth Duke) might well be proud of it, and of all the exterior which Salvin restored under his orders.' So wrote Sophy Louisa Percy Bagot in her 1901 reminiscences, *Links with the Past*. She first visited the castle in 1837 during the 3rd Duke's reign, and was a first cousin of the 6th Duke.

For the new Duchess in 1995, the Prudhoe Tower was to prove crucial in making the interior of the castle into a family home. Not only did the tower provide the Family Kitchen area and a big sitting room in the Library, but also the next floor up was to become the Duke and Duchess's bedroom suite, with their children's bedrooms above.

'We are a very close-knit family. I wanted to make sure that where we lived in the castle I could shout upstairs and, as in a normal house, know that our children would hear me. So we chose the top of the Prudhoe Tower, with its seven bedrooms, as our family quarters – which had once been the Death Wing. That spooked me a little. There were black fireplaces everywhere – even the beds were black. Katie's room was the "laying-out room" and we found some ashes in a wardrobe that had been forgotten.'

The Duchess also wanted her own laundry room in the tower. 'It means if I need a quick turnaround I can do it myself. The main castle laundry is downstairs and outside, and I would hate not to be able to do our own bits and pieces if I wanted to.' Indeed I caught her younger son, back from university, dumping on his mother all his laundry – which she seemed more than happy to do for him herself.

THE DUKE AND DUCHESS'S SUITE

The Duke and Duchess's floor above the Library has six rooms, including a bedroom, dressing rooms and a big bathroom. In the 1850s configuration the 4th Duke always intended that these bedrooms would be the 'best bedrooms with family rooms'.

At the entrance to the suite is a painting of the Duchess done by Katrina Bovill in 2006. In the inner hallway of the suite are vast French oak wardrobes, part of which are early eighteenth century. The doors are elaborately carved floral and musical panels in the Regency style.

The Duke and Duchess's bedroom has all the hallmarks of late twentieth-century Colefax and Fowler, an interior design firm that epitomizes the best of elegant English style, with a firm eye on quality and above all comfort.

The walls in the bedroom are wallpapered in a famous Colefax fuchsia on cream design, trimmed at the edges with red braid. Victorian chesterfields covered in rose chintz linen make a cosy sitting area in front of the fire. Above the marble chimneypiece is an 1860 Victorian giltwood overmantel mirror, commissioned by the 4th Duke from his architect Giovanni Montiroli. The four-poster bed has George III circular fluted end posts; the dressings and curtains are in red silk.

The Duchess thinks she made a mistake with the curtains. 'That is a regret of mine. I think they should have been cream. I was told that it would be very cold if you had cream curtains. But it would have been fantastic and I should have done it. It was the first room we did – we had just moved in – and it was a lot of material, so I've kept them.'

RIGHT From the hall of the Duke and Duchess's six-room suite in the Prudhoe Tower can be seen a portrait of the Duchess by Katrina Bovill, 2006. The wardrobe doors display carved floral and musical panels in the early nineteenth-century Regency style.

LEFT The Duchess employed Colefax and Fowler in the late 1990s to reupholster their bedroom, although she now wishes she had cream not red curtains. Fuchsia fabric lines the walls. The dogs sleep next to the sofa.

ABOVE From 1995, the 4th Duke's 1856 Prudhoe Tower was to prove crucial in making the castle into a new family home for the current Duke and Duchess, providing not only the Family Kitchen area below and a big sitting room in the Library, but also new bathrooms, such as the one above.

She uses an early eighteenth-century silver-gilt dressing-table mirror topped by cresting with a Rococo cartouche enclosing the Percy badge and garter motto. The 1st Duchess probably used it. Her Louis XV scrubbed-wood armchair is upholstered in modern red damask.

Pictures in the room include an 1870s painting of the Inner Court by Lady Emily Susan Drummond and late nineteenth-century views of Bamburgh Castle, Seaton Point, Warkworth Castle and Alnwick by Anthony Graham, along with a collection of recent watercolours of Alnwick Garden.

A new bathroom was installed in what used to be a bedroom. 'The castle is not a museum; it is not cast in a particular time period. It is a building that is still alive, and we need to keep changing to keep up with the demands of use,' explains Robin Smeaton. In the bathroom is a Victorian giltwood overmantel mirror, c.1860, and a 1750 Louis XV scrubbed-wood armchair, plus some pencil-and-wash drawings by George Holmes showing different views of Alnwick Castle, dated between 1812 and 1813.

The walls of the Duke's dressing room are military scarlet with the woodwork painted in a faux-tortoiseshell effect using raw sienna, burnt sienna, burnt umber, crimson and black. He has an 1810 colour aquatint print entitled *Men Replacing Paving Stones Outside Alnwick Castle* and an 1873 watercolour of Lady Emily Susan Drummond at Northumberland House.

THE CHILDREN'S BEDROOMS

Up the emerald-green staircase of the Prudhoe Tower to the children's top floor is a romantic 1920s painting by Philip de László of their 'great-grandma', Helen, wife of the 8th Duke, and Lord Geoffrey Percy.

The walls of the children's floor are painted fresh pink and with a skylight this area is bright, the light helped by a large giltwood overmantel mirror, three-sided with massive clasps, commissioned by the 4th Duke from the Alnwick School of Carving. The plain stucco ceiling is white with mint-green highlights.

LEFT The Duke's Dressing Room. Unlike his brother and father he chose not to have a valet, being the sort of man who likes to dress himself and run his own bath.

ABOVE Above the Duke and Duchess's Suite are the six other bedrooms for the children and their guests, off this landing.

On the landing are a 1798 oil by Sawrey Gilpin called *Dutch Pugs*, and a second by a 'Follower of John Wootton' called *A Pug Dog and a Spaniel on a Terrace*. Given the controversy about pug breeding, it is intriguing to see a pug here, slim and with longer legs than we often see today. There is also a pair of fine white-painted George III armchairs by Walle and Reilly, which have charming oval backs with the Percy crest on them and caned seats. They were commissioned by the 1st Duke for Northumberland House.

The children sorted out their own schemes for their bedrooms. 'I would listen to them,' says the Duchess. 'Missy is girly and Katie is more of a tomboy, so their rooms are quite different. One is pink and one is dark red. My son Max is mad on his football, so his is just covered in football pictures. And George is very organized. I hope their rooms reflect them; certainly they chose everything that has gone into their rooms.' The Duchess employed Lucy Manners to help the children design the bedrooms.

Katie's four-poster bed was specially made by Beaudesert, and the bed curtains and headboard are in material from

Vaughan in a red-coral geometric design called Samos Red. 'The lights attached to the back bedposts, so that one is able to read more easily, are called Paris Lights from Robert Kime,' says Lucy, The room has a George III Harewood work table, c.1790, with a square top inlaid with a bewildering number of woods: zebrawood, rosewood, partridge wood, amboyna. Katie's mirror is Louis XV, the frame inlaid with brass and scrollwork, and the chaise longue is mid-Victorian. You would not guess from what you see that as well as possessing many other talents Katie is a trained garage mechanic. Among the framed photographs on her dressing table is one of Patrick Garner.

Melissa has coral-pink painted walls and a four-poster bed also from Beaudesert, with unusual carved undulating ribbon on reeded posts – reflecting the 1780 and '90s taste of Louis XVI with a hand-gathered pelmet. Trained as a professional tennis player, Melissa is mad about sharks, and has been dipped in a shark cage off the Cape coast to look at great whites – hence the plastic head of a shark to contrast with the Louis XVI look.

George specifically asked me not to photograph his room. It has a freestanding bath in it, plus a George IV mahogany breakfront wardrobe and a George II bureau in burr elm cross-banded in walnut. After studying geography at Edinburgh University, he went on to the University of Damascus; he speaks Arabic and is interested in thermal energy.

Like his brother, Max is university educated. He too has a freestanding bath in his bedroom. His mahogany four-poster bed has a straight pelmet dressed in a Baltic linen from Christina Van der Hurd's hand-printed range called Medallion Rows, in indigo. The curtains are in Flower Cut Out, also in indigo. Both are distributed in the UK by Tissus d'Hélène. The theme of indigo blue and stone is contrasted with masses of framed photographs of Newcastle United footballers. A cricket bat in Max's bedroom is a small indication of how sporty all these children are.

LEFT The Duchess employed Lucy Manners to help the children design their bedrooms. Melissa's, pictured here, is in coral pink and has a Louis XVI style four-poster bed from Beaudesert. In contrast, the plastic head reflects her enthusiasm for sharks.

ABOVE Up a twisting narrow stone staircase, at the top of the Prudhoe Tower, is the room once used to store the ducal flags, and now a Moroccan chill-out room only for the Duke and Duchess's children, tented in Manuel Canovas fabric. An inscription on this flagstaffed top tower states: 'Eleanor Duchess of Northumberland ascended this tower, January 7th, 1856.'

THE FLAG ROOM

The highest room in the castle is the Flag Room, where the ducal flags were once stored, near the mast. It is now a chill-out zone for the Duke and Duchess's children. 'This is a Moroccan-inspired room,' says Lucy Manners. 'The Duchess wanted to have a den just for the children. They chose this wonderful heavy stripe from Manuel Canovas from Paris, and we tented it. The room is bright, fun, and has squishy low sofas, which are perfect for after-dinner lounging. The only panic was getting the drinks up the tight turret spiralling dark staircase.' After a few post-midnight 'sherries', I'd be more concerned about coming back down it.

The Duchess thinks it is 'a really cool room' but is banned from it. 'God knows what goes on up there. There is a combination lock on the door and I think the children change it regularly so that I can never get in. So I leave it to be their private place.'

THE WARKWORTH CORRIDOR

This pale pink corridor starts near the foot of the staircase to the Prudhoe Tower and is on the second floor. It was one of the first corridors the Duchess renovated, in about 1998.

Just outside the door into it is a large three-sided parcel-gilt ebonized display cabinet, glazed and outlined with guilloche mouldings. With its sloping black tops, and glued to the walls, it looks rather peculiar, but shows off a fine collection of Bloor Derby porcelain. Robert Bloor took control of the Derby factory in 1811 and built a team of fine painters. The earliest Bloor Derby marks did not have a crown in the centre of a circle, as the marks did after 1848. The china here is from the earlier period, and is part of a dinner service that includes soup tureens covered in 'Sèvres' flowers within blue circles, soup and dinner plates, and so on. There is also some Derby Imari.

En route to bed guests can enjoy looking at Landseer's

Coming Events Cast Their Shadows Before Them: The Challenge (1830s/40s), a large painting of a massive bellowing stag, lit by moonlight, and clearly in the rutting season. Sir Edwin Henry Landseer painted another stag swimming towards this big fellow, in answer to the challenge.

The corridor displays a fine aristocratic art collection with subjects that are mainly dogs, horses, family, saints and property. The 3rd Duke was especially keen on his horses and, as we saw

---

BELOW LEFT A fetching detail of a stool, one of the castle's rare surviving pieces of painted Gothic Robert Adam furniture commissioned by the 1st Duchess in the 1760s.

BELOW RIGHT There are numerous painted George III armchairs by Walle and Reilly here and on the children's floor. They have charming oval backs with the Percy crest on them, and were commissioned by the 1st Duke for Northumberland House.

RIGHT The blush-pink Warkworth Corridor, on the second floor above the state rooms, was one of the first corridors renovated by the Duchess in about 1998. Six of the rooms are guest bedrooms.

in the Duke's Study, on the artist James Ward, so there is an oil of a grey Cossack horse floating in a trot, given to him by their hetman, Count Platoff; with a castle-esque folly in the distance, this looks as though it was painted a few miles from Alnwick Castle. More magical is another Ward oil, *A Persian Stallion in a Gateway* (1820s). The stallion has mad, nervous eyes and with a fanciful and *capriccio* view of Alnwick Castle behind it, you imagine you are in Turkey. Dogs are well represented by an oil by John Boultbee (early 1800s) of Tycho, a favourite black retriever of the 5th Duke when he was a young man. There is a good painting of an American wolf dog by the late eighteenth-century Sawrey Gilpin, perhaps more famous for his oils of horses. This was probably bought by the 2nd Duke, who fought in North America during the American War of Independence.

There is an important sixteenth-century Giulio Romano (at least attributed to him) of a Madonna, hands clasped in prayer, and Child, on her lap, interacting with a saint. There is also a copy of the famous *Feast of the Gods* by Titian and Bellini, which was part of the Camaccini Collection but was sold during the First World War by the 7th Duke. The original is now in the National Gallery of Art in Washington.

At the end of this corridor of art is a fine eighteenth-century view of Northumberland House next to what is now Trafalgar Square. The picture appears to be in Canaletto's style but is thought to be by the equally talented Samuel Scott, who was renowned for the accuracy of his urban landscapes. In it we we see on the top of the grand town palazzo the lead Percy lion that is now on the back of Syon House. The Duke thinks that one of his Percy ancestors had a row with a monarch and had the lion turned round so that its bottom faced Buckingham Palace.

LEFT The corridor displays a fine aristocratic art collection of stags, dogs, horses, family, property and saints. From top, left to right: *Coming Events Cast their Shadows Before Them: The Challenge*, by Sir Edwin Henry Landseer, 1830s/40s, painted for Lord Algernon Percy, later 4th Duke; *The Cossack Horse*, by James Ward, c.1816, of a stallion – floating in a trot in a field near Alnwick – that belonged to the hetman Count Platoff, a gift to the 3rd Duke; *A Persian Stallion in a Gateway*, by James Ward, c.1820, with a view of Alnwick Castle beyond; *An American Wolf Dog*, by Sawrey Gilpin, late eighteenth century, owned by the 2nd Duke, who fought in the American War of Independence; 2nd Earl of Beverley's (later 5th Duke) black retriever, Tycho, by John Boultbee, early 1800s.

ABOVE AND FOLLOWING PAGES The Green Damask Room has a Victorian baronial border castle atmosphere, aside from a English Rococo 1760 George II giltwood ornamental mirror (above), one of a pair; the gilt cartouche frame is designed as bulrushes supporting flowers. The George III silver-gilt wine cooler by Paul Storr (overleaf) is one of a pair.

THE GREEN DAMASK ROOM

This emerald-green room feels Victorian. Above the chimneypiece is a Victorian mirror commissioned by the 4th Duke from his Italian designer Montiroli. The freestanding cheval mirror is William IV, often confused as Victorian for obvious reasons. The mahogany four-poster bed, the wardrobe and even the 'kneehole toilet' table are all mid-Victorian too.

Two portraits here celebrate the Percy lineage from a second son. One is of the 1st Earl of Beverley, the son of the 1st Duke and Duchess, in a black coat and white cravat, and the other of his countess, Isabella, painted by Joshua Reynolds in 1789 in a white dress and black cloak. A pair of fancy and very good 1760 gold gilt cartouche wall mirrors on either side of the bed liven up the room, as do the embroidered Chelsea Textile-style bed dressings. The faux-fur rug on the bed increases the baronial castle atmosphere.

Though north-facing, the room is not cold – a fact for which, as Robin Smeaton explains, we have the Victorians to thank. 'The most interesting device is the double window. It is a Victorian secondary glazing system, where you have two sets of sliding sashes. It is very, very quiet. When we were opening these fireplaces up an RAF jet went past on a training exercise. No sound came through the window but the noise down the chimney was horrendous. The majority of the castle's rooms have this double window arrangement.'

Not that there is a radiator in any of the bedrooms here. 'The Victorians also designed shutters, which along with the heavy interlined curtains make the castle surprisingly thermally efficient,' Robin explains. 'Her Grace was quite happy just to provide these coal fires which are in fact gas-lit.' Every aspect was considered in the renovation, including safety. 'Each bedroom's chimney was lined with a new stainless-steel liner flue, and carbon monoxide detectors switch the fire off should any fault occur.' And for convenience, a switch next to the wall light switches turns the fire on, or off, in an instant.

THE WHITE ROOM

Suitable for a singleton, this sweet little bedroom is called the White Room, but for no obvious reason. The drawings in this room include eighteenth- and nineteenth-century portraits of Maria, Countess of Coventry, Elisabeth, Duchess of Hamilton, Emily Percy and Isobel Percy. Along with the typical upstairs mix of Victorian, Georgian and Louis XV furniture is a fetching George II carved-wood oval mirror, crested with a shell. It was probably made for the 1st Duke and Duchess in about 1755.

THE BURGUNDY ROOM

The star here is the crowned giltwood Louis XV polonaise bed. However, the room was not always quite so dramatic. 'I made one big mistake on the interior design in the castle – right here,'

LEFT The White Room has a good 1755 painted mirror, and a green upholstered sleigh bed, suitable for one. There is a connecting door to the Burgundy Room.

ABOVE One of the Duchess's much loved stuffed dogs lies by the fire in the most dramatic bedroom in the castle, her favourite of all the bedrooms she has redesigned since 1995. The chairs are covered in gold Milton Damask from Claremont Fabrics and Furnishings.

the Duchess says. 'When we arrived this was a very dark bedroom – and I thought, I have got to lighten this up.' So in 1998, Charles Hesp painted this room pale beige with a strawberry frieze below the cornice, and there was a Hugh Mackay carpet with a strawberry border. The room was called the Strawberry Room.

'But it didn't work,' says the Duchess. 'You can't make it artificially light. Better you go with the dark.' She turned to Lucy Manners. 'My new brief was purple. I wanted a really dark black, purple and gold room. If you are staying in a castle for a couple of nights and you have got this *Phantom of the Opera*-style room with stuffed animals lying around it is a theatrical experience.'

Lucy Manners sent the Duchess five different bed-dressing samples. The Duchess, liking the dramatic, picked material from Sabina Fay Braxton. It is a type of deep burgundy velvet in a pattern known as Marie Antoinette.

She then chose a gold fabric for the two armchairs, which is Milton Damask from Claremont Fabrics and Furnishings.

Charles Hesp was sent the fabric choices and suggested painting the walls in a rich red. He grained the woodwork in a walnut effect. The Duchess decided that the family's William and Mary black-japanned furniture would sing here. Examples include a X-stretcher dressing table and a 1690 cushion-frame mirror, decorated with gilt chinoiserie. By the door two Rococo-style gold mirrors, in cartouche frames, are the 1st Duchess's, made in about 1765 in the manner of Linnell.

Proud in his peer's robe and wearing the Garter chain is her husband, Hugh, the 1st Duke, painted by Joshua Reynolds. In addition, there are two portraits by Thomas Philips. One is of their son, Hugh, the 2nd Duke, also in a scarlet tunic with his Garter Star pinned on it. The second is of Hugh's wife, Frances, the 2nd Duchess, wearing a white turban, ropes of pearls around her breast and pearl tassles on her shoulder and a black Empire gown.

THE RED BATHROOM

The en-suite bathroom to the Burgundy Room continues the dark red theme. Inside the nineteenth-century Chinese export games table, with its dragon feet, is a lovely mother-of-pearl-inlaid chessboard. A dressing table with an oval mirror is Chinese export lacquer.

ABOVE Almost all of the bathrooms are en suite, and the English baths in the castle are freestanding, restored and dating from the early twentieth century.
RIGHT To dress the Louis XV polonaise bed, the Duchess chose a hand-gaufraged devoré dark burgundy velvet from Sabina Fay Braxton, in a pattern known as Marie Antoinette. It is said that Sabina's clientele includes the character of Dumbledore in the Harry Potter film series. The 1690 William and Mary black-japanned dressing table and mirror, by the left-hand window, fit in well in this atmospheric bedroom.

THE BOWOOD ROOM

This room has one of the best guest bedroom views in Alnwick Castle. It looks out left to the James Adam's bridge over the River Aln and at the Capability Brown park.

The room's name derives from Bowood House in Wiltshire, owned by the descendants of the 1st Earl of Shelburne. John Fowler discovered a white rose chintz at Bowood in the 1950s and it was later made by Colefax and Fowler from around the 1980s. Here, on the walls and bed dressings, we can rejoice in this now-hard-to-find retro chintz. The subtle chintz colours are whites, greys and greens on a vanilla background.

The Queen slept in this room in 1982 when she came to Northumberland to open the Kielder Dam. A curtain was put across the Warkworth Corridor to give the Queen and her husband, Prince Philip, a private suite of rooms down this end of the corridor.

Sweet drawings of duchesses hang from the walls, namely Elizabeth, Duchess of Argyll, who looks like a young Queen Victoria, and Harriet, Duchess of Sutherland. The latter hangs

LEFT Elizabeth II slept in this bedroom in 1982. The retro chintz rose wallpaper and fabric is Colefax and Fowler, in a pattern called Bowood.
ABOVE A romantic view, created when the 1st Duke employed James Adam to design the Lion Bridge over the River Aln when the previous one was destroyed in 1771, in a flood. Capability Brown designed the landscape.

above the chimneypiece behind a grand sage-green Sèvres balustrade vase, which porcelain scholars describe as 'pâte-sur-pâte on celadon ground'. The handles are in the shapes of coiled snakes and the vase is decorated with a scene of Venus and cherubs. It is kept company by a pair of smaller but similar Sèvres vases on either side.

The four-poster bed is George III and its fluted head and cabriole legs are now painted pink and white. By the bed is a torch, as in every bedroom in the castle – provided in case of power failure. The fireplace here used to be in the Burgundy Room's bathroom, as the Percys treat fireplaces as chattels. The 1710 bureau is Queen Anne, made of burr walnut; the giltwood sofa is mid-Victorian, the chest of drawers is George II and the giltwood armchairs are Louis XV, made in the 1750s. The brass mirror is topped by a ducal coronet and the cypher 'EN', for Elizabeth Northumberland, the 1st Duchess.

Next door is a little bedroom with an Edwardian single bed, which is handy for the luggage, a valet or one's other half, if one's not in the mood to share the four-poster.

THE CHINTZ ROOM

The interior designer Robert Kime helped the Duchess carpet and upholster this pale cream-yellow room at the end of the Warkworth Corridor towards the end of the 1990s. The effect is elegant and restrained.

The Louis chairs are in off-white satin damask and the curtains are made of a Near East embroidered bottle-green wool. The four-poster bed is dressed in a delightful green chintz, set off by two plain banana-yellow plain vase lamps on bedside tables. These are cylindrical short cabinets, made by the Victorians to hold the bedroom 'piss' pot.

Above the grey marble chimneypiece is a small but fancy early George III giltwood overmantel oval mirror, with side plates, made for the 1st Duke and Duchess in 1765. The frame is carved as waterleaves topped with two birds. To the right dominates a French carved-oak wardrobe with elaborately carved Regency-style doors, similar to the ones in the Duke and Duchess's suite.

The best painting in here is of the vital Percy heiress, an innocent-looking Lady Elizabeth Seymour painted in 1739 by Allan Ramsay, when she had just married Sir Hugh Smithson, and holding a gouache drawing. There is a portrait of their daughter-in-law Isabella, Countess of Beverley, who married their second son and from whom the current Duke descends. The artist is Jacques Laurent Agasse. There is also a painting here

of Elizabeth Seymour's grandson Hugh, the 3rd Duke, with his wife, Charlotte Florentia, standing by the seashore.

The adjacent bathroom is famous for a serious leak. This occurred when the Duke's elder brother, film-mad Harry, had the actress Barbara Carrera to stay. She is famous as the James Bond girl in the film *Never Say Never Again*. Her bath

ABOVE A leak from this bathroom, during the 11th Duke's time, caused much damage downstairs in the Red Drawing Room.
RIGHT In the late twentiethth century, Robert Kime advised the Duchess on upholstery in this bedroom. It is east facing, at the far end of the corridor, and therefore perhaps the most private.

overflowed and the flood saturated part of the grandest room in the castle, the Drawing Room, directly underneath. 'Never again' was the motto in the castle thereafter, as Robin Smeaton explains. 'None of the baths at that time had overflows, so all the original ones that we have in the castle were sent off by the current Duchess to be replumbed and re-enamelled. The very large baths that we have are Victorian, going back to the 4th Duke's restoration. They have the up-stand plungers in them. We have only got one bath left to do now, which is at the very top of Prudhoe Tower.' I've used that bath, and can tell you that it is a huge, deep, cast-iron monster of a tub. Companies such as Drummonds still make these plunger waste systems – now with clever overflows.

THE LOVAINE CORRIDOR

You will not find much blue inside the castle, but you will here in the Lovaine Corridor because of the water pictures on the walls. And, of course, there is a good teaspoon's worth of royal blue blood in the Percys' veins via Josceline de Louvain, son of the Duke of Brabant, who married the heiress Agnes de Percy in 1168, and who gave the corridor its name. The walls are stipple painted a sea-green-sage-blue. The Duchess chose this colour to best display the naval, sea and lifeboat pictures collected by the 4th Duke, as well as oils of river views bought

by his grandmother Elizabeth, the 1st Duchess.

The display includes two of Duchess Elizabeth's paintings by Jan van Goyen, dated 1646: one of a tollgate on a dyke and the other depicting a river landscape with a castle on the bank. She bought these paintings on her Grand Tour travels in and around the Duchy of Brabant.

There is a print called *Lifeboat*, from the Royal National Lifeboat Institution, detailing its President 'His Grace Algernon George, Duke of Northumberland'. The lifeboat is probably one of the boats whose new self-righting design he sponsored and later had made.

Also displayed are two of Algernon's 1863 oils by John Wilson Carmichael. One shows a dramatic night scene of the Ramsgate lifeboat going to rescue the crew of a vessel wrecked on Goodwin Sands. The next shows the rescued men, women and children being drenched in the frenzied sea as the rescue boat rows into the Ramsgate harbour entrance. The nineteenth-century view of the town is well detailed in the distance. At the end of the corridor is a detailed engraving of 1745 showing a south-east townscape of eighteenth-century Newcastle and the River Tyne, and houses built along the top of the bridge.

The Lovaine Corridor contains a mammoth and, as the Duke would say, 'gaudy' cabinet, commissioned in 1855 by the 4th Duke to complement his new Italianate interiors. John Webb supplied it. It is quite over the top and accordingly was intended for the Drawing Room, before being replaced later by the Cucci cabinets. Technically speaking it is a 'Victorian breakfront *meuble d'appui*', the latter a French catch-all term for many types of cupboard or chest of drawers. The overall design is more Napoleon III. The frieze is made of cast gilt-brass in an acanthus design, above ebony doors inlaid with a marquetry design of a vase and flowers. Two gilt brackets are in the shape of a male atlantis and a female caryatid. An 1800 Chinese gilt-lacquer tea caddy painted with the Percy arms sits on top.

LEFT The bedroom corridor is named after Josceline de Louvain, who married Agnes de Percy in the twelfth century. He descended from Emperor Lothair I and Duke Reginar I of Lorraine, who founded the Lovaine dynasty around AD 900, later known as the House of Brabant.

ABOVE Two of the 4th Duke's 1863 oils by John Wilson Carmichael, one (left) showing the Ramsgate lifeboat going to rescue the crew of a vessel wrecked on Goodwin Sands, and the second the survivors returning to Ramsgate harbour. The 4th Duke was in the Navy and President of the Royal National Lifeboat Institution.

THE PAINTED BEDROOM

Made tickety-boo by the Duchess, this happy green, yellow and pink bedroom is the epitomy of 1920s ducal English country-house style. For an outdoors family who are the opposite of flamboyant, it is decidedly 'decorated'. The room's colourful ingredients come from all quarters, the most important ingredients being contributed by the Duke's grandmother, Duchess Helen. She and her children hand-painted on the ointment-pink walls vibrant flowering trees, perhaps Chinese camellias, bamboo, butterflies and exotic Asian birds, all underplanted with low hills and prominent yellow and blue irises above the skirting. In the far corner of the room, they each signed their initials in 1936.

Maybe Duchess Helen wanted to bring flowers, and something of the outdoors, inside, as you cannot see a formal

LEFT The accomplished 8th Duchess, Helen, and her children started painting this bedroom in 1936.
ABOVE The Duchess loved Duchess Helen's interpretation of the eighteenth-century Chinoiserie wallpaper and asked Charles Hesp to conserve and extend it, including into the bathroom.

garden from the castle, as the Alnwick Garden is a fair walk away. As the current Duchess comments, 'You have a view from some [rooms], but more often must climb up to see out of the windows. There isn't a lot of natural light here, so in the summer it can be oppressive. You can never tell what the weather is outside. If it is 30 degrees outside or minus 8 you don't know – you have no idea because the castle is a constant temperature.'

When the Duchess took on the castle, she fell in love with Duchess Helen's interpretation of eighteenth-century chinoiserie wallpaper and asked Charles Hesp both to conserve and to significantly extend it. He did this in such a way that it is impossible to tell what is by him and what by the 1930s crew. In addition, Charles painted the blue sky and cloud-painted ceiling.

Lucy Manners says that she did not do much in this bedroom, 'except a little tweaking on a shade or recovering an armchair in Claremont fabric'.

Most of the upholstered armchairs are late nineteenth or early twentieth-century English examples, with odd quirks, curves or buttoning, or chic faded gilt legs, not commonly seen in the shops today. The Duchess deserves enormous credit for getting everything out of the Percy storage and having it all restored, beautifully upholstered and in use once again. The Louis XV armchair by Lebas and the eighteenth-century giltwood settee on cabriole legs here are examples. Particularly fine are the late seventeenth-century gold mirror above the chimneypiece, which is Franco-Flemish, and the dressing-table mirror in brass gilt, topped by a ducal coronet with a 'EN' cypher.

THE PAINTED BEDROOM'S BATHROOM

You won't find any cold clammy bathrooms here, or taps that require a PhD in plumbing in order to extract dribbles of hot water.

I have stayed in a few castle bedroom suites but this room was my first and I can't imagine anywhere better in terms of comfort in the world. The smaller details hit home: the huge fluffy towelling robe, the thick white towels, the instant hot water, the bedroom wicker basket of headache, indigestion and you-name-it pills, potions and what have you on offer if needed. The magnified illuminated mirror is handy for the ladies or for the men if you want to examine each pore. 'No worries' if you forgot your bar of soap: as in each and every

bathroom there are lashings of lovely bath-time treats, such as Jo Malone's Lime Basil and Mandarin Bath Oil. Everything in the guest rooms, from the bedside books and latest magazines to the torch and bottled mineral water, is well considered. Understated in the chicest sense, but warm, generous, sparkly clean and extremely comfortable, it is Ritz-like, but better.

THE PINK ROOM

This is the plant-pot bedroom. The interior decorator Robert Kime restored the four-poster bed here and dressed it in his Jardinières Cotton, a French *fin de siècle* classic chintz that the Duchess particularly liked, featuring charming blue-and-white Chinese pots on a dove-grey background. The bed has fluted head and end posts, with a scrolled and carved decorated canopy – painted beige with blue painted decoration. The posts have egg-and-dart decoration on top.

The bed itself was saved on the advice of Robert Kime, who believed it to be an early example of Robert Adam. Shortly after inheriting the dukedom, the Duke asked the Duchess to oversee a forthcoming Sotheby's sale that had been planned by his older sister, Lady Victoria, when his brother Harry was alive. 'A friend recommended Robert Kime to me and said he would know about furniture, which is not my forte.' Going though all the items marked for sale, Robert advised her to withdraw a great deal from the sale, telling her that although in bad repair much was extremely valuable and her children and heirs would never be able to afford to buy it back. 'I had to be really tough and go over people's heads and say, "Sorry, we are withdrawing." The catalogues had been printed when I made the last withdrawal. I was already unpopular, and at the last minute, Robert said, "Save these beds." This again put me on the spot, but I kept thinking, I am paying him to advise me and I should take his advice. Apart from the one here, another bed is in the Chintz Room and a third upstairs in the Rose Room. What Robert Kime did was invaluable – I have so much to be grateful to him for.'

Lucy Manners was brought in later to finish many bedrooms.

RIGHT In the late 1990s the Duchess employed Robert Kime to advise on furniture and some upholstery. He believed this four-poster bed to be an early example of Robert Adam, so it was properly restored. It is now upholstered in his Jardinières Cotton, a French *fin de siècle* classic chintz of blue and white Chinese pots on a dove-grey background that the Duchess particularly liked.

'That bed set the tone of the room and so I did the rest of it around it,' she says. 'The sofa is in Cunard Weave from Claremont and a chair is in another Robert Kime material called Oak Leaves. The bedside lights are new and came from Vaughan, with specially made shades.'

There is a lot of William IV furniture here, including a giltwood oblong wall mirror, a footstool and a giltwood and gesso bevelled plate mirror. The rest of the furniture here is a mix of George I, such as the walnut concertina-action card table, and George III, including the oak bureau, mahogany dressing table and chests of drawers. Much of this was made for Stanwick Park. The earliest furniture is another concertina-action walnut card table, this one Queen Anne.

The Pink Room has two oils of the 4th Duke. One was painted by William Owen in 1810, when Algernon was a youth with scruffy fair hair, white cravat and a high-collared coat. The second is by Francis Grant, painted almost forty years later and showing him as Duke, wearing peer's robes over his naval uniform.

THE LILAC ROOM

This is the last of the three bedrooms on the Lovaine Corridor and a favourite of Dowager Duchess Elizabeth.

Here you could be in a well-upholstered genteel English rectory. Lucy Manners says that Charles Hesp painted the marquee-beige walls. 'The curtains are a copy of a French toile which is now out of print. The twin single beds were specially made and covered with a Pierre Frey material. The white woven bedspreads came from Chelsea Textiles, as did some cushions in the room.'

The pictures are rather too good for a rectory bedroom and fine enough for most people's drawing rooms. One is a 1746 portrait by William Hoare of Frances Thynne, Lady Hertford and later Duchess of Somerset, looking radiant and sympathetic. As we know, Frances's daughter was Lady Elizabeth Seymour, later the 1st Duchess.

FAR LEFT The Lilac Room has 100 per cent Siberian goose-down duvets and pillows, and sheared sheepskin mattress toppers, sourced by the Duchess's head of household Patrick Garner, who died in 2010. He was instrumental in helping the Duchess restore the castle and took care of every detail.
LEFT Hung above the beds are two paintings by Thomas Gainsborough, of the Hon. Henry Drummond and (below) of Lady Elizabeth Drummond, 1770–80s, grandparents of Louisa, 6th Duchess.

None of the Drummond inheritance and chattels that Louisa Drummond brought to the family on her marriage to the 6th Duke is in the state rooms, but many are tucked away all over the private side. One of these here is a Thomas Gainsborough portrait of the Hon. Henry Drummond, born in 1728. The fourth son of the 4th Viscount Strathallan, he is shown in a white wig with two curls over his ears in a peacock-blue velvet coat (1770s–80s). A second Gainsborough is of Lady Elizabeth Drummond, showing her powdered hair dressed high. His portrait of her brother, Charles Compton, Earl of Northampton, is upstairs in the Damson Room and that of his only daughter, Elizabeth's niece, showing her as Lady Elizabeth Cavendish after she had married into the Devonshire family, is in the Secretaries' Office.

THE HOTSPUR CORRIDOR

On the staircase up to the Hotspur Corridor, which is above the Lovaine Corridor, you pass a Battle of Waterloo-related ensemble collected by the 2nd, 3rd and 4th Dukes. Thomas Phillips's portrait of Napoleon Bonaparte painted in 1803 is matched by George Dawe's portrait of Arthur Wellesley, Duke of Wellington, sketched for a portrait owned by Tsar Alexander I. It was purchased by the 4th Duke to keep Napoleon company.

Aside from Wellington, another hero of the Napoleonic Wars was a Russian general and commander of the Cossacks whose portrait hangs here. Everyone at the time – including Earl Percy, shortly to become 3rd Duke – longed to meet Count Platoff. He was a much-feared general whose Cossacks became famous for harassing the French forces during the fight against Napoleon's invasion of Russia in 1812, in the midst of winter, despite the invader's superior numbers. The Earl acquired not only this painting of Count Platoff on his favourite charger but also the horse itself (see page 138). The horse would have been a greatly prized and much valued gift. In this painting, by James Ward and Thomas Phillips, the Count is wearing black uniform, silver epaulettes and a plumed black shako.

This corridor used to be known as the Nursery Corridor, from where – up on the third floor – children could be neither seen nor heard. By 1995, when the Duke and Duchess moved in, work was needed in the rooms on this floor, as Robin Smeaton explains. 'Before the Prudhoe Tower was redesigned the family moved in up here. But it was diabolical – there was plaster off the walls, there was no heating system and overall it was pretty grim.' In the 1950s, a time of post-war austerity, the housekeeper had simply gone off to Woolworth's, bought fifty

thrifty rolls of wallpaper and stuck the wallpaper up throughout this floor. The Duchess is more diplomatic, saying that when her husband was a child here 'It was very nice and homely but just different. It was for the children, but expectations have moved on so much from fifty years ago.' In addition, she points out, when Salvin redesigned the castle in 1850s the Prudhoe Tower was designed to house the state bedrooms and the key bedrooms were along the Boudoir Corridor and what is now the Archive Corridor, all on the first floor.

Now newly painted, carpeted and restored, the corridor holds a few Georgian chairs that came from Stanwick Hall. More art is displayed. The 1st Duke is here, displaying his Star of the Garter, again – this time in a drawing by Hugh Douglas Hamilton, showing the full powdered hair. Another picture here by an unknown artist of the English School (1769/70) belonged to his wife, Elizabeth, who called it 'Mr Cowslade in Van Dyck dress'. He was the tutor to their second son, Lord Beauchamp, later 1st Earl of Beverley, and he chaperoned him on his Grand Tour. Her grandson Hugh, later 3rd Duke, is along here, painted as a boy by Richard Cosway in the 1790s.

Those interested in medals and the illustrious Victoria Cross will like Gustav Pope's portrait of Major-General Lord Henry Percy, VC, a son of the 5th Duke. He is wearing a dark blue uniform with many decorations, his VC and a plumed hat.

The last picture is of military interest too, a portrait of an American colonial loyal to the Crown called Roger Hale Sheaffe, by the American-born Mather Brown (late 1790s). Sheaffe was born in Boston into a large family but his father died in 1771 when he was about eight years old. Lord Percy, who fought in the American War of Independence before he became the 2nd Duke, thereafter paid for the family – including Roger's education and first commission into the British 5th Regiment of Foot. Roger later became a British general.

The Duke puts the comfort of the guest bedrooms down to the good living enjoyed by our transatlantic cousins. 'Funnily enough, it is having American shooting parties that really made us refurbish all the rooms, because they are quite particular.'

RIGHT There are four guest bedrooms off the Hotspur Corridor, which is on the third floor, directly above the Lovaine Corridor. The Duchess has upgraded the entire floor except the Duke's old playroom.
FOLLOWING PAGES The Damson Room. The Northumberlands relinquished ownership of numerous properties in the nineteenth and twentieth centuries, which meant that the Duchess did not have to buy any new furniture and has sought to bring much out of storage, including the old-fashioned armchair here, newly upholstered.

THE DAMSON ROOM

The new upholstery in here was chosen, Lucy Manners explains, to complement the Grand Tour portraits. 'The curtains are in a material from Hodsell Mackenzie, the four-poster bed is a new one made by Beaudesert, and the bed curtains and pelmet are made in a material by Braquenie called Le Grand Corail Camaieux.' Aside from the Georgian and Victorian furniture, there is a more valuable William and Mary walnut cupboard made in 1690 and a 1750 Louis XV stool covered with silver flower damask. All quite cosy.

Here the 1st Duke, Hugh, pops up again – one loses count – wearing his Garter Star and sash, this time by Gainsborough. Otherwise, the bedroom pays homage to Pompeo Batoni, a Roman portrait artist much loved by aristocrats on their Grand Tours. One portrait by him is of Charles Compton, 7th Earl of Northampton, from the collection at Albury Park. Another larger Batoni portrait of the Earl, dated 1758, is in the Fitzwilliam Museum in Cambridge. The Earl and his wife died in Italy in 1763, he aged only twenty-six. They had one daughter, whose portrait is in the Secretaries' Office on the Boudoir Corridor, and her grandmother, the Dowager

Duchess of Beaufort, brought her up. These paintings came to the castle via the 7th Earl of Northampton's sister, Lady Elizabeth Compton, who married Henry Drummond, whose heir Louisa became the 6th Duchess of Northumberland by marriage.

Another Batoni here, dated 1769, is of the 1st Duke and Duchess's second son, Lord Algernon Percy, later 1st Earl of Beverley, wearing a green coat and waistcoat. Typically, Batoni painted the sitter with a bust in the background and in the distance a Roman temple or ruin, and pet dogs were encouraged to join the pose; but in this room the Batonis are just 'head and shoulders'. Lord Algernon's son was later to become the 5th Duke, and is therefore a direct ancestor of the current Duke.

THE DAMSON'S BATHROOM

Wherever possible the Duchess likes to place the bath in the centre of a bathroom – as we see here. Having stayed in this suite, and ever curious about one's plumbing, I asked Robin Smeaton how there always seems to be instant hot water. He explained that the boiler is under the Chapel cellar and 'fires hot water around the whole castle, on a pumped circulation like a loop, which keeps hot all the time. The problem we have is that when the house is full of guests the people who unfortunately lose their water pressure first are the Duke and Duchess, because they are at the highest level. They know that if their guests disappear off to have a bath they will have to go twenty minutes later. With hindsight being a great thing, we should have looked at having a stand-alone system specifically for the Prudhoe Tower.'

Aside from the bath, the room has a grand Louis XV marquetry coiffeuse made in 1760. The inside reveals a mirror, compartments and a jewellery drawer. There is also a large Anglo-Flemish seaweed marquetry walnut cabinet made in 1690, with elaborate inlaid doors. It rests on a stand with six tapering octagonal legs with waved stretchers known as bun feet.

ABOVE The portrait of Algernon, 10th Earl, is after Van Dyck, early to mid-seventeenth century.

RIGHT The curtains for this new restful en-suite bathroom come from Hodsell Mackenzie. The Louis XV marquetry coiffeuse by the window was made in 1760.

THE ROSE ROOM

'I think Nanny and I shared this room,' the Duke says. 'Until I went to school, I suppose at eight.' Child-rearing and this room have since changed entirely. The bed now shares the room with a bath. And a loo. The Duchess thinks this open arrangement is the best thing, especially for her sons, and even for modern couples. She is more concerned about space and light than having each component boxed off.

The bed is in the French style, and the curtains, Lucy Manners says, 'are a Rose Bernal material called Garden, which is distributed in the UK through Claremont. The screen hiding the bath is also in this material. The headboard is in Vine from Chelsea Textiles and the bed valance in a check from them too.'

Jessica Haynes from *World of Interiors* stayed here when we shot the castle in 2009, and was particularly impressed by the painting by Francesco Zuccarelli called *Jacob's Flight into Canaan*. It was on the 1st Duchess's List of Pictures. Known now as a eighteenth-century Rococo artist, Zuccarelli was Italian but made a few long trips to England, where the nobility fêted him and one assumes the sociable Duchess Elizabeth.

There is also a good pastel drawing from the studio of François Boucher of Madame de Pompadour wearing blue with flowers in her hair, and a Lewis aquatint of the Allies entering Paris past the Place Louis XV to the Champs Elysées after the 1814 defeat of Napoleon.

RIGHT You can't see it, but to the left of the bed is a freestanding bath, behind a screen. Rather than make a poky, windowless bathroom, the Duchess prefers such open arrangements, and her sons George and Max each have a bath in their bedrooms too.

THE FRENCH ROOM

At the end of the Hotspur Corridor is this charming little bedroom. The only deprivation is the lack of its own bathroom, so one has to pad down the corridor to where Charles Hesp has decorated a new masculine stand-alone bathroom, with mahogany, which overlooks the courtyard.

The 'French' label derives from the prints displayed here. Notably one of Napoleon Bonaparte, after Meissonier, dated 1811. This is actually a lithograph printed on silk, and signed 'Edwin Law'. Another print is of a mezzotint engraved by Wagstaff of the Duke of Wellington (1841).

BELOW A cosy bedroom for two friends at the end of the Hotspur Corridor. The white bobbly bed covers came from Chelsea Textiles.

RIGHT One cannot underestimate how fascinated British society was with the Duke of Wellington and Napoleon after the Napoleonic Wars. These prints and engravings relating to the two leaders were collected by the 3rd Duke.

THE OLD PLAYROOM

In between the Rose Room and the Damson Bedroom is a secret-looking door. This takes you up a tight spiral stone staircase into a room that seems to sit by itself on the castle roof.

Wallpapered in Woolworth's finest, c.1950, the room is cold, dry, a little dusty and jam-packed with boxes of old toys. There is a post-war electric bar in the fireplace, which was how rooms in the Hotspur Corridor were heated fifty years ago. Indeed, most of the rooms in the private side were still like this in 1995 when the Duke and Duchess arrived to live here with their young family.

This was 'our playroom', the Duke says, opening a mahogany drawer. 'I don't think anyone has been in here since I was playing soldiers. My elder brother Harry and I were mad on the American Civil War. He would have Union soldiers and I would have Confederate soldiers, and we would line them up and fire peashooters at them. Those are the original peas

that we would shoot,' he says, finding some dried peas in the drawer. 'And here is a train set and one of our old forts. I must come and sort all this out one day.'

BELOW The entrance to this old nursery is up a very narrow twisting stone staircase, and the room feels as if it sits up on the roof above the Hotspur Corridor. The room has remained untouched since the 1950s.
RIGHT ABOVE AND BELOW The toys of Harry, 11th Duke, and Ralph, the 12th and current Duke, are a reminder of these brothers' happy childhood, and a poignant memory for the Duke, for Duke Harry died aged forty-two in 1995, from heart failure after an overdose, thrusting his brother and sister-in-law into the position of 12th Duke and Duchess.

BEHIND THE SCENES

THE ARCHIVE CORRIDOR

Off the south-western side of the Keep from the Boudoir Corridor is a suite of private apartments that Salvin designed in the link from the Keep to the Middle Gateway. This houses the Collections and Archives Department. Colin Shrimpton, the archivist until 1999, called the archives held in the Record Tower the 'hidden soul of the estate' (in an article in the estate's newsletter, *Percy News,* quoted throughout this section). The Duke of Northumberland's archives are some of the largest in a private house in the UK and contain many items of national significance. The Duke employs three full-time Collections and Archives staff and it is one of his favourite departments.

The suite of rooms, dating from 1854 to 1864, has interconnecting doors, while a plain corridor runs alongside for staff. Originally the Duke and Duchess's bedroom was in the centre, with both a dressing room and sitting room on either side. Today the service corridor running alongside these rooms is used as an informal gallery in which to store pictures, many of which are in the process of being catalogued, about to go off to be repaired or simply not wanted elsewhere. The pictures include an oil of the 8th Duke by de László, a drawing of the 6th Duke when he was a boy, and a photograph taken in 1902 of the horses and state coach, which the 7th Duke had redecorated for the coronation of Edward VII. There is also a list of names of those at Alnwick Castle who served in His Majesty's forces during the Second World War. They number about sixty-five men, from the estate office, park farm, household and the draining, game, gardens, masons, stables, motors and woodmen departments. Many were taken prisoners of war and four were killed in action, including the 9th Duke.

LEFT The 4th Duke knocked out the 1st Duchess's Adam chapel and library and built a suite of rooms for himself and his wife, including this former boudoir, now the Manuscript Room.

ABOVE The Manuscript Room in the late nineteenth century, when it was the Duchess's boudoir. The grand gold Italianate ceiling is copied from the Camera Borgia at the Vatican. The mirror is now in the Private Dining Room.

THE MANUSCRIPT ROOM

If you were inclined to be nosy, an archive room such as this would keep you amused for days on end. Scattered around here are all sorts of curiosities. There are, for instance, a piece of plank inscribed 1857 from the Second Restoration; a Ministry of Health map of 1939 detailing how the castle turned into a boarding school, with what is now the Private Dining Room becoming a classroom and the Duke and Duchess's Studies small dormitories; and a gold ink bottle and case for a pen used by Major Henry Percy, brother of the 5th Duke, when he was ADC to the Duke of Wellington at the Battle of Waterloo.

Robert Adam's library for the 1st Duke and Duchess took up this and the next two adjacent rooms, before Salvin made

this room the 4th Duchess's boudoir. With a width of 26 feet/ 8 metres, it is well proportioned, with a rich and ornate gold ceiling carved of pinewood in an Italianate design taken from the Camera Borgia in the Vatican. Originally, the walls were hung in orange silk damask. The chimneypiece is of white marble and, unlike most of those in the state rooms, inlaid with *pietre dure*, executed at the Royal Manufactory in Florence. Plaques of coloured marbles portray birds, fruit and flowers on a background of lapis lazuli and porphyry. The sculptured heads in the chimneypiece are the work of Signor Nucci.

A significant archive collection of the papers of the 4th and 6th Dukes is housed here. Listed by the Historic Manuscripts Commission in 1872, they were bound into books. 'The next stage is to evacuate them from here in the Manuscript Room and take them down to the Record Tower, where we have much more stable controlled conditions and humidity,' says Christopher Hunwick. He is the archivist but, taking a swipe at preconceptions, he says he 'never wears a dusty cardigan'. He looks after the Duke's paper and parchment collections and is responsible for the modern records.

LEFT The bookshelves in the Archive Office. Modern record keeping is extremely important to the estate.

ABOVE Curiosities abound in the archives, including (left to right) 1835 papers belonging to the 3rd Duke; coins reputed to be from the rule of Optimus Princeps, Emperor Trajan, AD 98–117; and the gold ink bottle and pen case worn and used by Major Henry Percy when he was the Duke of Wellington's ADC at the Battle of Waterloo (1815) .

THE ARCHIVE OFFICE

Next door to the Manuscript Room is the office of the archivist. There is still a great deal to be done in terms of cataloguing the archives. 'We rely on the nineteenth-century solicitors' listing, but over my lifetime I will try to catalogue the Syon collection to modern standards,' Christopher says. This is about a sixth of the Duke's collection and contains the earliest Percy material, including a charter of King John, dated 1200, with his seal on it. Some of the most important documents are the original purchase deeds for the castle, together with their royal seals.

Looking after all the archives is an immense task. 'We need to control the paperwork from the modern-day work on the estates, for historic but also legal, auditing, and health and safety reasons. A comprehensive system of modern records management was introduced for the estate in 2007 by Clare Baxter. Our job is to identify significant invoices such as for work on a painting as opposed to the milk bill for the office.

'We also get a constant stream of genealogical requests, and can sometimes find things out for them, but with Percys all over the world, we don't have much relating to cadet branches of the family.' Christopher's prime duty is to supply items needed for business, such as clarification of rights of way or legal information required for archaeologists' surveys. The Duke's recent restoration of the castle's hydro-electric scheme required research on nineteenth-century technological history.

'A nice side of the job is the steady stream of researchers coming in. I can suggest that they might want to try looking here or there. Often researchers add to our knowledge of the collections, so it's a symbiotic relationship.'

THE COLLECTIONS DEPARTMENT'S OFFICE

The ceiling of the Collections Department is white stucco; the room was once the 4th Duke and Duchess's bedroom (see page 27). The department's job is extensive, as Lisa Little, who is in charge, explains. 'We serve the family, estate and the general public on behalf of the Duke. We provide provenances, help with exhibits and organize loan requests, which come in from cultural institutions around the world.' Another responsibility is fulfilling the Duke and Duchess's ambitious conservation objectives, using the latest research. The Duchess says: 'I don't get involved, as they know when to do things and have their own schedules. Every year the chandeliers are taken down and cleaned. Everything is done, even the books in the Library. They come in and they clean it for about a week – just working their way around those library shelves. They are all very professional.'

The task is extensive, costly and ongoing. Much has already been achieved. Even if it ended now, the Duke and Duchess's tenure will be remembered for this achievement. A large team of people deserve credit for it, as Lisa indicates. 'We have regular visits by painting, ceramic and metalwork conservators, and a bookbinder steadily repairs between sixty and eighty books each year. We use reports from our oil painting conservators to prioritize which artwork requires immediate attention and so on.' The project is funded by what the Duke calls his 'chattels fund', created by some of the proceeds from the sale of the *Madonna of the Pinks*.

THE STORAGE ROOM

In any house, cupboard space is often an issue and Alnwick Castle is no exception. 'We don't have enough storage here in the castle,' the Duchess says, which is why her aim is 'to have every single piece of furniture that is in storage – most of which is at Syon or in a warehouse – used somewhere'.

Here are numerous Georgian and Victorian pieces, lots of old lamps and needlework glass-panelled firescreens, silver-gilt candelabra, unused gilt stools or chairs from suites of the 3rd Duke's 1822 gilt Morel and Hughes commissions, the 1st Duchess's set of George II red walnut dining chairs from Stanwick Park, and much more.

Anything out of storage faces another issue: the Duchess loves moving the chattels. 'Since I was a child I have moved furniture around. My parents used to say that when Father Christmas came he would never know how to find the bed because I moved it three times a week.' In this respect the Duchess thinks she was impossible to work with when she first arrived at the castle. 'Furniture would be put down somewhere and then they came along and stuck a label on it. But I moved every single piece of furniture ten times, including paintings, until I was happy. I was very difficult. Now there is a new warehouse we use as storage and I want to get everything out and see what we have got. I hope it will all be used in the Syon House restoration – one of my next big projects.'

THE TEXTILE ROOM

Along with the storage room, this room was once the 1st Duchess's chapel. The textile archive is stored rather than on display. Some of the most interesting items are the military uniforms and servant livery, in the Percy colours of blue and yellow. There are also hunting clothes that belonged to the family, and boots and hats of all descriptions. Aside from what is in the wardrobes, there are piles of archival cardboard boxes, stuffed with tissue paper, under which one can peek at a few items. The waistcoat and silk jackets of either the 2nd or the 1st Duke are here, with exquisite embroidery, even on each silk-wrapped button.

In one box are Duchess Helen's 1937 coronation robes. Instead of the loose cape worn by peers, a peeress's robe is made of velvet and fitted like a long dress but open down the front and with short sleeves edged with fur. Under this she wore a lighter dress in gold. The rules at a coronation are that the monarch has a 6-yard/5.5-metre train, made in hand-made purple silk velvet and trimmed with 5-inch/12-centimetre

---

ABOVE This eighteenth-century jacket of either the 1st or 2nd Duke, in immaculate condition, displays exquisite hand-embroidered silk weaving.
RIGHT The nineteenth-century Percy staff uniforms hanging here were last worn in 2011, when the state coach was used at Lady Catherine's wedding.

18 June 1815. With little wind, crossing the English Channel was slow, but on landing, he travelled at speed in a chaise and four horses to Whitehall – three of Napoleon's gold eagles (symbols of his First Empire) sticking out of the carriage's windows, being too big to fit inside – and arrived with the great news on the evening of Wednesday 21 June. The Prince asked if many were dead, and Henry answered, 'The loss has been very great indeed,' upon which the Regent burst into tears. After widespread fears of defeat, the victory caused 'great agitation' throughout London that night, and 'many ladies fainted' as the news spread of the great loss of life and numbers of wounded. One of Henry's family, Miss Frances Williams Wynn, recorded in her *Diaries of a Lady of Quality 1797 to 1844*: 'I remember the great dark stain on his uniform; the horror I felt, in the midst of all the triumph and joy of the moment, when he told me, in answer to my questions, that it was the blood of an officer killed close to him. Still more when I heard him tell how, in taking off his sash as he undressed, he shook from the folds fragments of the brain which had lodged there.'

THE RECORD TOWER

Standing at the eastern extreme of the castle all by itself is the Record Tower. Inside, hidden technology and protection make for perfect conditions. Colin Shrimpton says it has a 'smell, stillness all of its own' and describes its contents as the 'bible of the estate'. In the late twentieth century, after an estate worker, Gordon Wilson, had installed a new gallery and created more space in the tower, most of the family's archives were moved to Alnwick, the family's headquarters, and the Duke's sister, Lady Victoria, helped bring the art collections from various ducal houses under one administration.

London fires were historically a great hazard, and some books and manuscripts kept at Northumberland House and now at Alnwick were damaged by fire in the eighteenth century – a Bacon manuscript, for instance, has singed edges. Riches are of no use unless you can prove ownership, a maxim the 2nd Duke had in mind when in 1812 he poached the new archivist at the British Museum, Joseph Strutt, to look after the Syon records house. Colin Shrimpton explains that 'from then on care of the records became a watchword of family policy'.

Canadian ermine. A duchess is allowed a 2-yard/1.8-metre train, also with 5-inch/12-centimetre ermine edging, while a baroness is allowed a 1-yard/0.9-metre train with 2-inch/5-centimetre edging. Black sealskin spots designate rank. When the Archbishop of Canterbury places St Edward's crown on the head of the new monarch, the peers put on their crimson-velvet-lined coronets trimmed with ermine. Duchesses' coronets are in gold with eight strawberry-shaped leaves creating the 'spikes' on the circlet.

Military history is tucked away in another special box that contains the uniform worn by Major Henry Percy, brother of the 5th Duke, when, as ADC to the Duke of Wellington, he carried the Waterloo Dispatches to London. This was the first news of the Allied defeat of Napoleon, which he gave to the Prime Minister, Lord Liverpool, and to the Prince Regent. Henry left with Wellington's written account of the victory in a lady's satchel only hours after the battle had ended on Sunday,

ABOVE The archivist, Christopher Hunwick, outside the Record Tower.
RIGHT Inside the Record Tower the atmosphere is perfectly controlled with the most advanced technology. The tower holds 'the bible of the estate'.

THE HOUSEHOLD ROOMS

While the Keep holds the state rooms, chapel and private rooms, there are only a handful of rooms in the Keep for the household. In part, this is because neither the Duke nor Duchess has a valet or a ladies maid; and the butler does not live in. The servants' quarters were on the outside of the curtain wall, on the south side, near the middle gateway. These rooms are now occupied by the American students from St Cloud State University, Minnesota. 'It is better for buildings if they are used,' says the Duchess. 'Since 1981 the university has done an exchange and an International Study Programme. England is one of the places you come to and you live in this wing of the castle for a term.' Indeed, ever since the Second World War, parts of Alnwick Castle have been used by various schools and colleges. From the students' online blogs it is clear that they make the most of their free access to the Alnwick Garden.

Male servants all slept in the gatehouse, stable staff on the upper floors around the coach yard. Today, very few of the staff sleep anywhere in the Keep, which is for family and guests.

Colin Shrimpton, the former archivist, records that 'At the end of the nineteenth century household staff numbered 86. There were 39 women, with 6 laundry-maids, 6 housemaids, and 6 kitchen maids as well as personal and travelling maids. Of the 47 men, 4 were footman and 16 were coachmen and stablemen.' According to the 1913 instructions for Christmas presents the most important, or 'upper' servants, were the housekeeper, cook and ladies maid, followed by the groom of the chambers and the Duke's valet, then the under-butler, heads of laundry, still room, etc. and lastly, the footmen and 'Other Maid Servants'.

By the time of Ralph's father, Duke Hugh, the number of staff was much smaller. The household is well described in Jeremy Musson's book *Up and Down Stairs* in an interview with a long-serving member of the maintenance staff called Graham Luke. When he joined the staff at the age of fifteen there were about ten staff, but in the 1970s that number went up to twenty-five. He remembers Duke Hugh and Duchess Elizabeth as being 'very regal, and part of a much more formal life'. Mrs Renwick was the housekeeper: 'Very grand. She was an epitome of a housekeeper, tall, large, dressed in black, and she ran everything,' Duchess Elizabeth remembers. For Graham Luke Mrs Renwick 'was next to God . . . she was a demon'.

The duties of housekeeper are now divided between the staff. The Duke and Duchess have both a butler and a household controller, and eight daily ladies. To dust and hoover the castle yourself would take two weeks, if not more, and imagine changing the sheets in eighteen bedrooms, let alone doing the ironing and washing. In addition, there are two secretaries, a few general household helpers, a cook, a security team and someone in charge of the garage and cars.

Not technically part of the household – or as the Duke and Duchess call it, the family department – the Northumberland Estates office near the stable block is the workplace of about fifty people. Here you will find property surveyors, planners, PAs, accountants and bookkeepers, and people working in human resources, health and safety, forestry, grounds maintenance, fencing, marketing, tourism and retail. Then there is the farming department, and twelve people who work in the game department. And of course, the head agent. The Collections and Archives team work in the Keep and the Alnwick Garden is a charity run and financed separately by a trust.

When I got to know the castle more than a weekend guest would, I developed a sense of living at boarding school, with the Duke as housemaster and many people busy here and there. At the same time, the ducal household does not feel extravagant, for it is obvious that help is needed to live here – not only to run it properly and in comfort, but also to allow both the Duke and Duchess to pursue their own lives as a married couple, have quality time with their children and entertain. They also need time for their business and extensive charity commitments.

In the hall at the staff entrance door is a board with all the staff names on it, twenty in total, so that you can tell who is in or not. Typically, it looked half and half to me. Asked how the family creates a sense of privacy, the Duchess replies, 'You don't really, apart from in our kitchen. I found it difficult the first year because we have a diary and anyone who gets it knows where we are at any one time.'

While at first the Duchess found that intrusive, she is busy with many projects and often away. Also on becoming Duchess, she soon recognized that delegating much more would suit her and everyone else. 'If a big house party is arriving the butler will need to know what time guests will be arriving, where they are sleeping, what they are eating and so on. There was no way I could have done that all by myself and continued to develop my other interests. I gradually saw that you couldn't live or manage Alnwick on your own. Nor

RIGHT Once laid with lino and a little glum, this Kitchen Corridor and the staff floor were the first area the Duchess renovated after 1995. A mass of happy family holiday snaps are framed along the walls.

can you wander around in your pyjamas at night and have a blazing row because you might bump into a security man at two in the morning. The collection has to be protected and everything comes at a price. You adapt.'

Just as the household has always risen to the occasion when royalty visits Alnwick Castle, so the staff excel themselves four times a year when the Duke and Duchess rent out the castle for grand shooting weekend parties. It was the Duke's idea. 'It was one way of helping to pay towards the annual cost of the shoot and it is quite good for the house to be used to the full a few times a year,' he says.

'It was a house that was always used for entertaining,' explains the Duchess. 'Eighteen guests come at any one time. We very much include them. They do the table plan and we ask them not to put us at the head of the table – it is their party. We email menu choices and organize the wine they want. The household controller will run all that and make sure from the minute they arrive they have the best possible experience. A lot of planning goes into it. We are lucky because people want to come here and we don't have enough weekends free for more. So we can do it on our terms and the people are all fascinating and lead interesting lives – I quite enjoy it.'

In the beginning, there was a 'guest incident' and some rudeness, so the Duke and Duchess sat down with the household controller. 'We said to him, "Do we really want to carry on doing this? It doesn't bother us." Funnily enough, Patrick Garner said yes. He gave us three reasons. The first one was that the castle was cleaned up to a standard it wouldn't be for us. Two, the staff liked the wonderful tips, which go into their Christmas bonus. And I think it was also important for the shooting and the people on the estate to see that we are commercial, that we didn't have money to burn, and that we had to be sensible.'

Having been around at one such weekend, and seen all the silver gilt come out for the State Dining Room and grand Continental ladies dressed for dinner in long dresses and wearing good jewels, I can see that, for the house, it is the equivalent to taking a car for a thorough service and giving it a good run on the motorway. The Duchess is certainly proud of the staff and seems to thrive when the house is full of people and life at the castle is in the fast lane.

LEFT 'I was asked not to repeat this so will say it only once . . .' The chirpy yellow staff sitting room is the place to be if you want to hear any local or castle gossip. Geordies are famed for their excellent dry sense of humour.

THE STAFF ENTRANCE AND KITCHEN CORRIDOR

The entrance to the Kitchen Corridor is on the left as you walk into the courtyard. Delivery boxes, coats and boots lie around, and immediately on the right is an Italian cypress wood chest that came from Syon House. It was probably imported from Italy during either the sixteenth or the seventeenth century and would have been considered a luxury. Today it is likely to have a crate of mineral water plonked on it.

This corridor and the rooms off it were the first areas to be renovated after 1995. Afterwards, the Duchess put family photographs all the way through here. Ian August, who knew the austere condition of this area before 1995, says, 'It has been transformed to a quality that has never been there since it was first built. These places can just quietly go down but the Duchess's influence in the castle, and even on the Kitchen Corridor, has given everything a sudden lift up.'

THE STAFF SITTING ROOM

One of the staff, a lady, asked me what the title of this book was going to be. 'Fawlty Towers,' I replied, 'after all of you.' One of the delights of photographing the castle was chatting to the staff, who all have a cheeky sense of humour. This is the room they use for lunches, tea breaks and gossip. Needless to say, the staff work extremely hard each day keeping the castle visibly perfect.

Cleaning is a serious matter, a vital element in the care of the collection that has become much more scientific in recent years. Since the implementation of a conservation programme, many were told they were causing long-term damage. Therefore, here you will find a list of instructions on microfibre cleaning without chemicals, using the low-suction 'Museum Vac' for silks, how to apply Renaissance wax to metalwork or marble and other cleaning methods. Polishing the furniture is carried out only every five years, as the wood gets a 'milky appearance' if the job is done too frequently. Pony brushes are used for giltwood dusting, hog's-hair brushes for marble and plasterwork, and so on. The last instruction on the list is 'If in doubt, leave it'.

The supervisor of the household ladies, Linda, told me what she and all the other household ladies get up to. 'It gets especially dusty once the visitors come, so we work daily before the castle opens at 11.00 a.m. The carpets have to be hoovered every morning too, or the wooden floors dry mopped. Fortunately the windows only have to be cleaned twice a year.'

Occasionally a visitor causes raised eyebrows. One visitor walked around munching a huge flaky pastry sausage roll in the State Dining Room, leaving crumbs everywhere. Another year a used nappy was found stuffed behind a painting in the Red Drawing Room. 'The biggest pain is finding chewing gum chucked on to a state room carpet.' Regarding the latter, such horrors are best dealt with by using an ice cube, by which I mean on the carpet not the perpetrator.

In the winter, when the family are in residence, everyone in the household 'mucks in' when the house is full of guests. Someone will replace the shampoo bottles, another person writes the name plates or 'door cards' for each guest bedroom. Ian, the chauffeur, helps bring in logs for the fires, which the household ladies set up during the day. The fireplace in the State Dining Room consumes practically a small tree each evening. The ladies sometimes work evenings when a dinner is on, by rota, helping in the pantry with the silver and china. All cleaning is done by hand. Alternatively, they may help serve the food. The State Dining Room is often used, but the Duke dislikes silver service, as it takes too long, so the food is served already plated.

THE HOUSEHOLD CONTROLLER'S OFFICE

The castle's aide-de-camp resides here. No aiguillettes are worn, but a good sense of military planning is required for the multi-functional duties the household controller performs. Andrew Farquharson, the current household controller, chose two oils from Northumberland Estates to decorate his office. One is of a cow called Lady Jane, painted in 1883, and the second is of a massive bull called Snowstorm, painted in 1877. Both were commissioned by the 6th Duke and Duchess, from the artist A.M. Gauci. Andrew shares the office with the butler.

The Duke recalls interviewing the previous controller, Patrick Garner, in 1995. 'I offered him the job of butler and suggested that he might find my family rather more casual than he was used to, to which he replied, "Well, Your Grace, if you are prepared to rise to my standards, I will come down to yours." Patrick became indispensable. He never dropped his standards, he managed houses and people, organized events, looked after our sick dogs and kept the wheels of our household moving.'

Previously Patrick had been butler to the Duke of Marlborough, at Blenheim Palace in Oxfordshire, but at Alnwick it soon became apparent that the role was more than that of butler, so the title household controller became more apt. 'He loved wine and encouraged me to "lay down" a fine cellar. When our children were growing up and some

ABOVE Andrew Farquharson, the uber-efficient household controller, hard at work. The Duchess prefers a household head controller to having a housekeeper. There seem to be few strata of management at the castle: trust, competence and good delegation are the form.

OPPOSITE Andrew chose the pictures for his office. This 1877 painting is of a massive prized bull named Snowstorm. Another one is of a cow called Lady Jane. These Alnwick Castle Dairy Shorthorns, kept at the Percys' Park Farm in Hulne Park, won both national and international acclaim.

were moving into their own homes in London, he liaised with builders and decorators, organized cleaners, and dealt with any problems. He ran all the family homes as well as Alnwick and dealt with lettings, catering and staff. Areas of the castle and Syon were being restored and he was an essential component of the restoration team.' It is clear that the Duke and Duchess miss him greatly since his sudden death in 2010. The Duchess was especially keen that this book remembers Patrick, as well his wife, Jane, 'who provided the essential love and support that made his life fulfilled and happy'.

No doubt it was daunting for Andrew when he took on the job late in 2010. On his office wall is a small note that says, 'Only Robinson Crusoe could get everything done by Friday.' At first he constantly heard how Patrick did it. But 'I am not Patrick,' he exclaimed to me. He had hardly 'worked out where the front door was' before he won his spurs, only months into the job, by successfully organizing the wedding of the Duke and Duchess's eldest daughter in 2011. An integral part of

any such Percy celebration includes a dinner for over three hundred people, all connected to the estate. This dinner, a couple days before the wedding, and of the same standard of hospitality as the wedding breakfast, was in itself a colossal event to organize.

Andrew reports to the Duchess on most matters; he describes her invariably as brave and trusting but adds that she 'misses no tricks and is absolutely *there*. She is thoroughly modern, says what she likes and just expects that it will be done to a quality and standard, without further interference. It is fantastic for me.' Nonetheless, the Duchess pays great attention to detail, and may change draft suggestions with 'What I think would be nice is . . .' The overall objective is that guests have a very good time and are comfortable.

THE BUTLER'S PANTRY AND SERVICE

This room is used to clean shoes, to store everyday crockery and for the staff to work in when the house is full of guests. When a dinner party is in progress, and once the main course has gone to the dining room, the duties of the pantry team are to clear all dirty glasses and ash trays in the Library, add logs to the fire, puff up the cushions, replenish soft drinks and spirits bottles, and refill the ice buckets. Once dinner is over the Sèvres or whatever china is used is carefully hand washed.

CASTLE KITCHEN

The Castle Kitchen, one of the first rooms to be renovated after 1995, is the domain of Gillian Millar. She is Scottish, trained as a cook at Edinburgh, and has worked for the Duke and Duchess since 1996, a year after Duke Harry died. She lives in one of the towers on the edge of the castle wall but follows the family up to Scotland for the summer months.

OPPOSITE The Butler's Pantry off the Kitchen Corridor was renovated in the late 1990s.

ABOVE LEFT A breakfast tray for a lady guest. Gentleman guests tend to eat breakfast in the Private Dining Room, where one can have a full cooked English breakfast.

ABOVE RIGHT Matthew, a local young man, a bright undergraduate and in his holidays the castle's part-time general factotum, coming out of the lift en route to a dinner in the State Dining Room.

She describes her style of cooking as traditional British, but light rather than heavy, and based on the seasons. Dinners can range from shepherd's pie to more exotic Thai dishes. 'The Duke loves his game, as do the children. I often pot roast pheasant as I find this the most succulent way of roasting it. I also cook pigeon, partridge and grouse. Grouse breasts are best pan-fried and done pink, while pheasant should be like chicken with the juices running clear.'

The shooting season clearly dictates the ingredients to some extent. Shoot lunches are often eaten at Hulne Priory in the park near the moors. Typically winter lunch menus include favourites such as coq au vin, beef stroganoff, lamb stew or meat and cheese fondue. Gillian is also very good at making tartiflette, a mountain dish consisting of layers of potatoes, crispy bacon, cream and chunks of reblochon Alpine cheese, all baked in the oven.

'They know about good food,' says Gillian, 'but like every family, they have their quirks. I don't cook using cream much or make a fuss about sweet things – they are not a big pudding family,' although for shoot lunches they like fruit crumble, sticky toffee pudding and bread-and-butter pudding. Straightforward English milk chocolate appears to be popular after dinner if one is watching the telly. 'Perhaps it is their genetics, but as long as I have known them they just take one portion and rarely a second. Ancestrally they are not a fat family.'

The kitchen only uses game that is shot on the estate. When she cannot source ingredients from Northumberland Estates, Gillian sources them locally or from British suppliers. Burnside Farm Foods, in the Scottish Borders, supplies Parma hams, salami and cheese. R. Turnbull and Sons, Alnwick, supplies her with the majority of the household's meat and eggs, as they are locally sourced; they have won many accolades for their products. T.R. Johnson, the butcher in Wooler, supplies her with dry cured bacon and locally laid quail's eggs. Again, she uses Turnbull for the castle's fruit and vegetables, which they get from local farms or from the Newcastle fruit market.

Northumberland is famous for its shellfish, and Robertson's Prime in Alnwick supplies the castle with crab, mussels and prawns. L. Robson and Sons supplies lobsters and the famous 'Craster Kipper', an oak-smoked herring from Craster on the Northumberland coast. Other fish comes from North Shields fish merchant, Frank Rourd. Fish caught by the Duke and other members of the family is used fresh; larger fish is smoked.

Turkey
Gammon to order.
BACON

Elevenses 10·30/10·45
@Abbey

Lunch - 12 /12·30 - Castle.

PHEASANTS → CASSEROLE
→ Duchess Eliz

FAR LEFT Gillian Millar is the Duke and Duchess's loyal and superb Scottish cook, photographed here in the midst of preparing the main course for a dinner in the State Dinning Room. Her style of cooking is seasonal, locally sourced, light and British.

LEFT The board in the Castle Kitchen indicates that Dowager Duchess Elizabeth will be served pheasant casserole for dinner.

THE HEATING ROOM

It is extraordinary to think that the Victorian heating system for the house worked by steam, and that even today state rooms are heated by hot air. 'The reason why it was steam was if you heat water to produce steam you can transmit an awful lot more heat than you can in hot water. The temperature can be really, really high,' Robin Smeaton explains. Today there is a ducted hot-air system. 'In the basement here are big heater batteries. Cold air is drawn in from the outside, heated across these batteries and air pipes, and then distributed by wall and floor ducts into the state rooms.'

From the second half of the nineteenth century the fuel was coal and the boilers were in the Alnwick Garden, which is quite far from the castle.

The hot-water boilers here in the cellar of the Prudhoe Tower, under the Chapel, were installed in the 1940s. They were originally fuelled by coal, and then converted to oil and latterly to gas in 2005 – with some very efficient condensing boilers, which are good at reducing carbon dioxide emissions.

THE LAUNDRY

The Laundry and the adjacent linen rooms, near the front door, were once bedrooms for the footmen. The only problem, especially when it snowed, was that their bathroom was across the chilly courtyard. Today these rooms house linen cupboards and washing machines. Mrs Richardson is in charge of the castle's laundry, which in scale and equipment might be likened to that of a small hotel. It is especially busy during the winter shooting season when bed linen and towels for eighteen guests are changed weekly.

Many of the Percy Irish linen napkins are well over a hundred years old, yet in perfect condition. Linen must be ironed damp. Fortunately, Mrs Richardson has an rotary ironer of industrial proportions that merrily irons damp laundry and vast numbers of sheets fairly quickly.

THE FLOWER ROOM

Seen in the photograph on page 191 at the end of a house party with a few untidy remnants, the flower room is a useful place for the arrangement of flowers. While the Alnwick Garden has its own greenhouse, the garden is a charity and not part of

LEFT The castle's linen is stored off the Inner Courtyard. The footmen's bedrooms used to be here in the nineteenth century and they had to run across the courtyard to the nearest bathroom. Today, very few of the staff sleep anywhere in the Keep, which is now only for family and guests.

Northumberland Estates, so oddly the castle does not have a dedicated greenhouse or conservatory; nor are flowers grown for cutting. The Duchess is keen at some point to start growing more potted plants, which when in flower could be wheeled into position in the castle. One of the difficulties is that the family live in the castle in autumn and winter which, until a greenhouse system is put into place, means that plants and flowers come from a florist.

There are no particular rules but in the winter months the Duchess might have yellow or lime-green flowering *Cymbidium* orchids in some of the state rooms, with the odd white gardenia here and there. Splashes of green might come from Boston ferns, peace lilies or big parlour palms. Red flowers stand out and look especially good. Yellow tiger orchids look good in the Drawing Room. Sometimes you might find large jardinières packed with pots of white cyclamen in the Library and dark pink phalaenopsis in the Ante-Library, contrasting against the blue silk walls. In the Lower Guard Chamber there might be potted white hyacinths or winter pansies, or just white orchids. Upstairs Liz, one of the guides and helpers, is very good at making posies for bedside tables.

The Duchess's florist in Northumberland is Caro Dickinson at Flowers Unlimited, based in Hexham. Caro provides flowers for special occasions in the castle, especially the grand shoot weekends. She specializes in natural garden-style flowers and the Duchess says they always look 'wonderful'.

THE STORAGE ROOMS

Aside from the general household provisions, the cellars store the tableware used in the state Dining Room (see pages 85–7). Much of this is either in cabinets or in wooden boxes. The latter were, until comparatively recently, used to transport the Duke's silver gilt on trains, following the family from house to house. One London and North Eastern Railway label on a box of silver cutlery details a trip from Alnmouth to King's Cross and is dated April 1988, the last time the Duke's father moved the family to Syon Park, as he did each summer; he died that October.

ABOVE What with weekly shooting parties throughout the winter, and the castle having room for the family and up to eighteen guests, the castle's laundry room needs to function much like one in a small hotel. All the bed sheets are professionally starched and ironed.

RIGHT Next to the linen storage room is the flower room, here looking a little dishevelled after a weekend's efforts.

The silver-gilt handled knives come from Dobson and Sons, 32 Piccadilly – goldsmiths and silversmiths to Queen Victoria. Much of the grand silver-gilt candelabra, vases and tableware was commissioned by the 3rd Duke and Duchess from Rundell, Bridge and Rundell between 1822 and 1830.

Silver gilt is not only less expensive than solid gold but also lighter and easier to move; moreover, the gold gilding does not tarnish as quickly as silver. This suited its original purpose: the Northumberlands' collection of silver gilt was in part commissioned by the 3rd Duke and Duchess to take to Paris for the coronation of Charles X in July 1825.

THE WINE CELLAR

Wines that are ready for drinking are brought here from storage on the estate. The wine cellar is stocked predominantly with French bottles – champagne, Bordeaux, Burgundy, Sancerre and Chablis – with the odd Sauvignon from places like New Zealand. The Duke is steadily buying wines *en primeur* (that is, still in a barrel) in order to get wines that may not be so easily available later. Prices tend to be lower than they are once the wine is bottled and released on to the open market; moreover, fine wines from small estates tend to sell out during the *en primeur* campaign. The difficulty is that you have to wait so long before you can drink it, which is, of course, the pleasure for some. The cellar is also well stocked with spirits.

LEFT Stored in the cellars, the silver-gilt handled knives come from Dobson and Sons, 32 Piccadilly, goldsmiths and silversmiths to Queen Victoria.
ABOVE Engraved on a silver-gilt tray is the belt of the Order of the Garter surrounding the shield of the Duke of Northumberland in the coat of arms.

FOLLOWING PAGES
LEFT Much of the grand silver-gilt candelabra, vases and other tableware was commissioned by the 3rd Duke and Duchess from Rundell, Bridge and Rundell between 1822 and 1830.
RIGHT The Duke offers rather good wine, most of which he buys from France.

SALVIN'S KITCHEN

'Aside from the chapel, the only important interior the 4th Duke did let Anthony Salvin do was the kitchen, which is in the grand medieval kitchen style,' says the Duchess. The objective in siting the kitchen south of the Archive Corridor and Middle Gateway along the southern curtain wall was not to have smoke or food smells too near the Keep.

Though medieval in style, Salvin's kitchen had all the latest Victorian mod cons. Colin Shrimpton describes it as 'spectacular', designed 'with a hydraulic lift capable of raising a ton of coal to fire the roasting spit and ovens. To speed up delivery of food from the kitchen to the State Dining Room, an underground passage was constructed to connect the two. The kitchen even employed an engine man.'

Shortly after it was built in 1854 a newspaper report on the 4th Duke's annual workmen's banquet for a total of 640 guests spoke with wonder of the kitchen chimneys, which 'smoked as if the structure was on fire', and described the scale of the catering. 'A huge baron of beef was at the fire. Numerous other joints were before the principal range, all upon spits turned by a water wheel of considerable power.' Charcoal stoves were glowing, grates were hissing and steam was escaping from 'the coppers in which various joints of beef and pork were being boiled'. The baron of beef, which would have weighed about 350lb, was cooked from nine o'clock in the morning to half past four in the afternoon, 'done to the bone, but not in the least burnt on the outside'. The workmen appreciated that 'other Dukes in opening their new kitchens would order a great dinner for their own friends, but he does it for us'.

Now the American students from St Cloud State University in Minnesota use this kitchen as their dining room.

THE ESTATE OFFICES

Alnwick Castle is not just a family home but also the heart of a modern business called Northumberland Estates, whose offices are alongside the south-west corner of the castle's outer

LEFT Salvin's 1850s kitchen, commissioned by the 4th Duke and Duchess, was the most advanced of its day. It is now the dining room for students from St Cloud State University in Minnesota, who stay here as part of an cultural exchange programme.
ABOVE The reception area of Northumberland Estates, the heart of what is a modern and now diversified business, which underpins the entirely privately funded conservation and running of the castle.

curtain walls, next to the Clock Tower and Stables.

The estate has some 120,000 acres/48,562 hectares of land under its stewardship, of which around 4,000 acres/1,618 hectares are commercially farmed in hand, with a further 10,000 acres/4,046 hectares or so down to forestry. The majority of the land is rented to farmers, many of whom have lived on the estate for many years, indeed for many generations.

Since the present Duke took over in 1995, the estate has diversified from its reliance on agriculture into many other areas including commercial property and development. This has helped play a role in the regeneration of Alnwick as a town, drawing in household names such as Homebase, Sainsbury's and Argos, all of which have helped benefit regional businesses in general. The estate fought for two years for planning permission to have twelve affordable houses built down the road at Lesbury, where the Duke's grandmother once lived, designed for local families. The estate also manages a residential property portfolio, as well as another visitor attraction at Syon House on the edge of London and the Albury Estate in Surrey.

This well-run business, helped by economic growth over the last twenty-five years, creates sufficient returns to plan and sustain a professional programme of reinvestment. While the Duke deserves credit for how he has transformed the estate, he says that none of their work in the castle could have been achieved without the revenue stream created by his 'skilful and determined' agent Rory Wilson. The Duchess adds that, 'Without long-term planning and good management you couldn't maintain the castle, renovate the rooms, conserve the art, or maintain the fabric of the building.'

THE STABLES

On passing through the Barbican and Gatehouse, you find yourself in the first courtyard of the castle's grounds, the Outer Bailey. If you turn right from the Gatehouse along the wall you come to an arch into the courtyard of the Stables.

In the Middle Ages, there were no buildings here, only a moat. The 1st Duke put buildings here but the ones seen today were redesigned by Anthony Salvin as stables around a courtyard between 1854 and 1865 and have not changed much since. On the east side are the estate offices and on the south side the 135-foot/41-metre-long Guest Hall, finished in 1863. On the west side were the stables, which are now the café. On the north side are two coach houses. One of these is today the shop. The other contains an early nineteenth-century coach, an 1850s landau, and the state coach, commissioned in 1825 as a gift to the 3rd Duke from George IV, built he represented the King at the coronation of Charles X in France.

The state coach was also used at Edward VII's coronation and in the Lord Mayor of Newcastle's coronation procession in 1953. More recently, it was restored to take the Duke and his daughter, Lady Catherine Percy, to her wedding at St Michael's Church in Alnwick in 2011. Katie, as she is known by the family, married Patrick Valentine.

LEFT The Duke and his eldest daughter, Lady Catherine, wearing a dress by Bruce Oldfield, in the state coach en route to Alnwick Church for her wedding in 2011.

ABOVE The coach was built in 1825 for the 3rd Duke when he represented George IV as special ambassador at the coronation of Charles X of France.

OUTSIDE THE CASTLE

THE LANDSCAPE AROUND THE CASTLE

Over seven centuries, the Percys have made many improvements to the land around Alnwick Castle. This chapter focuses on the River Aln and landscape seen north of the castle; then a quarter of a mile/400 metres south-east of the castle, behind trees, the Alnwick Garden; and lastly the ducal Hulne Park. The latter you cannot see from the castle, but from most of the state rooms the view north includes the Lion Bridge. To the west of the bridge is the 3-mile/5-kilometre-wide park containing a priory, tower and graveyard.

Perhaps the most important figure in the estate's history is Hugh, 1st Duke. On his wife's inheritance in 1750, he led an ambitious restoration of the lands, re-establishing Percy authority, which had languished in the preceding centuries. From the fifteenth century the Percys were in debt, and as being Catholics they suffered politically and economically under Henry VIII and Elizabeth I, the 7th Earl being executed in 1572. The 9th Earl avoided Alnwick, and the estate declined. In the vicinity of the castle, the land over the river had by the seventeenth century reverted to a mess of plots, with subletting and rack-rents benefiting neither the Earls nor those who worked the land.

Talented and shrewd, the 1st Duke overhauled the entire estate. He invited 'Capability' Brown to the castle in 1770, and three years later Brown's foreman was in charge of seventy-eight workmen, improving, among other projects, the entire view we see north from the state rooms and from outside the castle, as illustrated on page 202.

For those who wanted to walk out of the castle to the garden, or to use a carriage, the 1st Duke built a new gateway from the south-east of the castle's walls, called the Lion Gateway. From here, Capability Brown's men constructed an earth causeway to avoid the route going down and up the steep hill. Today this enables you to walk between the castle and east to the gardens without puffing.

LEFT I took this photograph of the castle early one cold winter morning in 2009. The Duchess was watching from her bedroom. Capability Brown widened the River Aln in the nineteenth century to calm down the river and enhance the reflection.

ABOVE Looking out of the Inner Courtyard towards the gateway of the Lion Gateway, in a winter snowstorm of 2010.

On the north side of the castle, the curtain wall was demolished to make a terrace to see Capability Brown's clumps of lines of beech trees in the park, north of the bank of the River Aln – an area known as the North Demesne.

A road along the river was diverted to run north in a large and hidden loop. The 1st Duke commissioned Robert Mylne, famous for his design of Blackfriars Bridge in London, to build the fine Denwick Bridge for this road. Part of the loop of this road runs alongside the far east side of the garden, near the Treehouse and garden car parks, northwards from the town over the Aln; this is today called the B1340. To celebrate the building of the new Mylne Bridge there was a feast in Alnwick town in 1768, for which was cooked a huge dumpling that fed two hundred people.

The 1st Duke employed the canal builder James Brindley to help Capability Brown improve the river. Brindley created a series of cascades along the river, upstream in Hulne Park, to slow it down, and he widened the river beneath the hill of the castle, giving a better reflection of the castle in the river, as you can see from the photograph on page 200.

Robert Adam's younger brother James then designed the Lion Bridge in 1772. This was decorated with a statant lion, copied from the Percy lead lion on Northumberland House (now on Syon House). The previous bridge was destroyed by a terrible flood in November 1771.

The 1st Duke's descendants made few changes to the area immediately around the castle until those made after the 4th Duke invited William Andrews Nesfield, his garden designer at Stanwick in Yorkshire, to 'give a report of his opinions as to the improvement of the views'. The castle's archives store Nesfield's recommendations and sketches of the castle from across the river. According to Colin Shimpton in his excellent book *A History of Alnwick Parks and Pleasure Grounds* (on which I have greatly relied here), Nesfield complained, for example, that the 'grandeur' of the scenery was spoilt by individual 'little shrubs' on the hill under the castle, which had self-planted and now looked 'spotty'. Tighter clumps of bushes but well spaced out followed.

More recently, since 1995 the Duke and Duchess have cleared fences around the immediate vicinity of the castle, which beforehand contained horses.

THE ALNWICK GARDEN

When the 1st Duke and Duchess restored the castle in the mid-eighteenth century, their efforts ere directed at the parks more than the garden, a quarter of a mile/400 metres to the east of the castle's walls. However, James Call is recorded as being in charge of a garden in 1756, having joined his relative Thomas Call, who was in charge of Hulne Park. It is unclear who built the garden, but at this time there was a walled garden where the Alnwick Garden is now, with espalier fruit trees, a vinery and a nursery in which to grow trees for the park.

In 1807 the 2nd Duke commissioned John Hay, a planner from Edinburgh, to make improvements in the garden and build new hothouses, including a fruiting pine stove in which to grow pineapples, and mushroom, vine and peach houses. As recorded in the memoirs of the Caledonian Horticulture Society, Hay applied steam to a chamber of stones below the 'bark-bed' of the hothouses – an extremely modern method for the time, although it did not work very well; he later improved it at Castle Semple in Scotland. New walls, a seed house and a house for the gardener were also built at this time.

From 1817, the 3rd Duchess, Charlotte Florentia, who introduced Indian buffaloes into Hulne Park, built a flower garden on the site of the current garden; she was 'an avid collector of plants'. The garden was extended in the 1860s when Anthony Salvin, employed by Charlotte Florentia's brother-in-law, the 4th Duke, redesigned the castle. The new Lion Tower and gateway between the Inner Bailey and the garden replaced the eighteenth-century one, but the path still used Capability Brown's causeway. A series of new hedges from the castle along this path created a 'telescopic' view towards the garden.

By purchasing more land from the town the 4th Duke almost doubled the size of the garden. In 1860, he asked W.A. Nesfield to design a new Italianate scheme for the garden with a central pond, conservatory, terraces and parterres. The 4th Duke died when the garden was half built, and there is doubt as

---

OPPOSITE On the left is the early 1300s Constable Tower of this medieval fortress, looking north over the River Aln.

ABOVE The Percy lion, with its straight tail, on the Lion Bridge, is a copy of the lion on the Duke's Syon House. This bridge was designed by James Adam when a flood swept away the old one in 1771. It is an example of a public project in Adam's castle style.

FOLLOWING PAGES The Grand Cascade of the Alnwick Garden, designed by Jacques Wirtz.

to how much of Nesfield's design was implemented thereafter. Italianate gardens were then in fashion: for instance, up the road at Chillingham Castle Sir Jeffry Wyatville was designing an Italian garden, while at Osborne House on the Isle of Wight, Prince Albert had, with Ludwig Gruner, just constructed terraces with ornamental parterres and statues in the Italianate style.

By the 1880s, the head gardener at Alnwick Castle, Thomas Ingram, was looking after a flower garden of 20 acres/8 hectares along with a kitchen garden of 7 acres/2.8 hectares. The flower garden was designed to be at its best in August, for the start of the shooting season, so the flower beds were filled with dahlias. A photograph of c.1900 shows a central grid of vast symmetrical rectangular beds sweeping past a modest lily pond up the hill where the Cascade now is. Between the flower beds were box topiary shapes of hounds, foxes and the Percy lion. By 1900, twenty-one people were working in the garden.

As happened in large gardens all over Britain, by the 1930s expenditure on the garden had been cut dramatically. During the 'Dig for Victory' campaign of the Second World War, the garden had a renaissance when the flower beds were put to use for growing food. After rationing ended, the glasshouses were demolished and the 10th Duke gave the entire garden to the woods department to use as a nursery for conifers, such as larch and spruce, destined for Hulne Park.

By 1995 the garden had fallen into total abandon. The newly arrived Duchess often took the dogs for walks here, in what had become a forlorn 'Christmas tree' garden, full of weeds, rubble, a car park and an old tennis court. It had its walls and mature trees but was otherwise derelict. Yet, she says, 'Even in such a state of dereliction, the garden was magical. It had beautiful bones, and because its beauty was so apparent, it was particularly tragic that it was unappreciated.' When her husband suggested that she might like to make a new garden, she was inspired.

She could have made a private garden and sought to restore the Victorian incarnation; or if restoration was in mind, she could have reverted to any of the designs of the last two hundred years. But for the Duchess there were other considerations, which influenced what we see today. The family spend October to April at Alnwick Castle and winter months are not the peak time for flowers, while visitors come to the castle in the spring and summer months. Another consideration was that her husband could not be less interested in formal gardens, being much keener on natural landscapes, wildlife and sport; he would rather walk the dogs round Hulne Park up to the moors than through clipped topiary. Certainly, the Duke did not need a restored pineapple conservatory or peach house in order to enjoy a slice of fruit at breakfast.

Significantly, the site is invisible from the castle. This allowed more design options – including the possibility of a contemporary style – than would not have been possible had the new garden had to relate to the castle's architecture. A deciding factor on how to design a garden in this space was its size. The old walled garden alone is a 12-acre/5-hectare site; the whole site is a vast 50 acres/20 hectares. In this pragmatic age, this was too big for a garden all to oneself. Just as she does not wish to sit in one of the castle's state rooms by herself and think, 'Isn't this beautiful?' the Duchess knew that the garden site would flourish best as 'a venue' and 'when full of people'.

Not only is her mother a great gardener but also she had her husband's family to inspire her. The 4th Duke opened his garden and Hulne Park to the public – a first for the duchy; he also eschewed Salvin's English interior designs for a bold Italian scheme that caused uproar in 1856 among English architects at RIBA, who questioned the 'propriety' of such a foreign scheme inside a medieval border fortress. She was particularly inspired by the 1st Duchess – who, like her, had married without any expectation of becoming a Duchess: she knew that the effort Elizabeth Seymour put into her new position as Duchess, 250 years earlier, had had a lasting impact on both the castle and the region. The present Duchess was conscious of the opportunity she had to use her new position to make a positive contribution in Northumberland.

The Alnwick Garden, therefore, was designed from the outset as a public garden in a contemporary style that aimed to be a national tourist destination. In addition, it was important to the Duchess that it appealed to the local community, and to young and old alike.

Her ambitions matched the region's economic needs. In 1996, certain areas of the United Kingdom were classified as deprived by the European Union and funds were available to these regions for iconic projects that would bring rural economic benefits. One such area was the north-east of England. So the Alnwick Garden project bid for European Union aid and was successful. The Duke made a significant contribution of millions of pounds.

To attract public funds and set up a charity, the Duchess had to say from the outset what the money would create. In addition, while great garden makers and designers of the past such as Gertrude Jekyll, Lawrence Johnston or Vita

RIGHT At the top of the Grand Cascade, to the left under the beech trees, purple *Primula beesiana* putting on their May display.

Sackville-West could more quietly plant gardens and develop them gradually, barely had saplings been planted than the Duchess had the unenviable task of getting the public to visit the garden immediately, and then year on year. Taking on the paraphernalia of modern marketing and public relations, and so sticking her head well and truly above the parapet, she rose to the challenges and boldly set forth.

Jacques Wirtz was chosen as the designer for the Alnwick Garden in mid-1997. Wirtz is a landscape architect world famous for his use of evergreen hedging in both swirly and straight patterns. One of his most noted designs is in his own garden at Schoten in Belgium, where big-scale formations of clipped rounded box trees mass together, forming an undulating cloud effect or, as he says, like a flock of green sheep huddled together. In all that Jacques Wirtz does, he has a reputation for being sympathetic to the history of a site, and combining this with innovative thinking and a great knowledge of horticulture. The contribution of his son Peter has also been important.

The decision to pick an overseas designer was unusual, as garden design in Britain is dominated by domestic talents. Nonetheless, commissioning the Belgian Jacques Wirtz had a historic resonance for the Percy family for, as we have seen, the 1st Duchess was passionate about her Brabant and Louvain ancestors and indeed art from the Low Countries (which include Belgium), and travelled there extensively.

The Wirtz master plan for the Alnwick Garden was a public statement, written to attract the public. Ian August, who worked alongside the Duchess at the Alnwick Garden Trust, was one of the first people to see it at a meeting with Jacques Wirtz and his son Peter, and he describes it in his book *The Making of the Alnwick Garden*. 'The central axis or "spine" was a three-tiered Cascade with a Lower Basin, flanked with topiary hornbeam hedges that would grow twenty feet or more in height. The hedges provided the green architecture, organizing the space and giving shape and substance – laying flesh on the axial bones of the hard landscaping. At the top of the mound was a walled ornamental Garden. Peter imagined it as a "hidden paradise" laid out in a repeating square design packed with colourful perennials, divided by rills, paths and fountains, and given an upward perspective with tall, pleached crab apples. That was the quiet area of the garden.' Below the Cascade, in the Lower Garden, 'everything was sinuous, organic curves with many different garden areas – the Serpent, Rose and Poison Gardens, the Quiet Garden, the Garden for the Senses – each offering their own atmosphere and surprises.'

The garden was opened to the public late in 2001, before being officially opened by its patron, the Prince of Wales, in September 2002. The Prince opened the second phase of the Alnwick Garden in September 2007. The Queen and the Duke of Edinburgh later visited the garden in June 2011, attending a party organized by the Duchess for carers and volunteers.

THE PAVILION

You enter the garden through the Pavilion, which is enormous, contemporary, bright and light, designed by Sir Michael Hopkins to bring the outside inside. Following modernist principles, Hopkins is considered 'one of the leading lights of hi-tech architecture' by RIBA, and is known for his innovative roofs. He also designed the fabric canopy, in conic style, around the opera house at Glyndebourne in East Sussex, and a pavilion in the gardens at Broughton Hall in Yorkshire.

The Pavilion looks from the outside like a transparent duvet. Inside, aside from having many uses, the building offers a panorama of almost the entire garden. In front of it there is tiled paving in which over six thousand fibre optic fairy lights, which change colour, are embedded in the grout between the tiles to give the effect of a field of stars at night. The building is wonderful at night, as the lighting is so clever, even in the loos, only I can't help wondering what classicists, such as the garden's royal patron, think of it.

THE CASCADE

From the Pavilion, the dominant view ahead is of the Grand Cascade on the garden's hill. The central water feature is flanked on either side in perfect symmetry by enormous hornbeam domed tunnels, in which there are windows so that you can see the Cascade and fountain as you walk up the steps within. Eight hundred and fifty hornbeams were planted, when the trees were ten years old. Above the Cascade, and enclosing the parallel hornbeam design, towers a quasi-semi-circular framework of tall mature chestnut, sycamore and lime trees, which were planted in the nineteenth century.

Every thirty minutes the fountains erupt into life. With synchronized gusto they start spouting at the top. Getting more fired up, they work 7,000 gallons/31,800 litres of water down the twenty-one weirs to the lower balustrade, where jets shoot water high up and over into the lower bowl. Then in the lowest pond, in a grand finale, an enormous fountain erupts like a water volcano.

RIGHT Queen Elizabeth II and the 12th Duchess of Northumberland at the Alnwick Garden in 2011. The Queen and Prince Philip had lunch at the castle and later visited the garden, attending a party, organized by the Duchess, for Northumberland's carers and volunteers.

In all there are 150 jets making the display.

At the top of the Cascade the mood changes. Water flows gently in pebble-based rills down to a pair of calm circular pools on either side of the Cascade, each curtained by a circle of fastigiate oak trees.

THE ORNAMENTAL GARDEN

The jewel in Alnwick's crown is hidden behind the trees at the top of the Cascade, in the old walled kitchen garden. 'The Ornamental Garden is the classic plantspersons' garden,' says the Duchess. With 16,500 plants, there is a lot to see and it is certainly my favourite spot in the garden.

The garden is asymmetrical, but in this masterpiece of Wirtz's design appears as a series of squares, giving a good sense of overall symmetry. A few of the squares are crossed with paths, creating triangular beds.

LEFT The central water feature is flanked on either side in perfect symmetry by enormous hornbeam domed tunnels, in which there are windows so that you can see the Cascade and fountain as you walk up the steps within.

ABOVE Above the Cascade, and enclosing the parallel hornbeam design, towers a quasi-semicircular framework of tall mature chestnut, sycamore and lime trees, which were planted in the nineteenth century – seen here in spring.

I make no apology for illustrating the garden more or less completely in late May and June. Every season in this walled garden brings various treats for plant lovers, but June is my favourite month for English gardens and if you had to pick one season to see this walled garden at its zenith, I'd recommend this bonanza period.

Two of the 4th Duke's Venetian wrought-iron gates have been restored to the entrance to the Ornamental Garden, with the central third and fixed panel being new.

In the centre is a square Islamic-style pond topped with black slate. Mysterious water blobs gurgle from its black depths, as if some whale creature is on its way up. From this 'source pool', rills lead to two symmetrical pools – each in a hedged 'room' – to round ponds on the hillside outside the walled garden. Paths in chalky white gravel make a light contrast against the box hedging that edges all the flower beds and borders. Around the central pond is oak trellising, covered in climbing roses and clematis. Lining the walls is an herbaceous border in which grow hybrid musk roses, tree peonies, shrubs, ornamental trees and a multitude of other flowers. Jacques and Peter Wirtz have planted these as blocks of single species, rather than repeating the same plant in numerous clumps along the bed. There are also a couple of dovecots in the garden.

BELOW LEFT Lining the walls of the Ornamental Garden is an herbaceous border with musk hybrid roses, tree peonies, shrubs, ornamental trees and many flowers. Here white delphiniums grow in front of climbing white and yellow roses.

BELOW RIGHT In the centre of the Ornamental Garden there is a square pond raised in Islamic style, its edges topped with black slate.

RIGHT Under the pleached tree squares and along the border by the wall, Wirtz's European modern block planting of flowers is ravishing. Clockwise from top: *Paeonia lactiflora* 'Pink Parfait'; *Primula capitata*; pink and white phlox; *Papaver orientale* poppies; classic peonies; *Primula vialii*; lupin 'My Castle'; *Astrantia major* var. *rosea*.

FOLLOWING PAGES

LEFT In the walled flower and water garden, at the top of the Cascade, beds of blue delphiniums at the entrance lead to the pond, rills and high oak trellising (above). Oriental poppies lend an intensity of colour (below).

RIGHT Jacques Wirtz used tall pleached crab apples to form repeating square rooms and give upward perspective (above). In May and June, peonies are a delight (below).

PAGES 216 and 217 Irises (left) and poppies (right) in the Ornamental Garden.

THE CHERRY ORCHARD

The annual cherry blossom festival is a famous event in the Japanese calendar. Now the arrival of spring in Alnwick is Japanese too, with masses of white blossom from some three hundred white *Prunus* 'Taihaku' cherry trees. The only orchard of its kind in Britain, it is a visual feast in April or May.

'The Cherry Orchard offers a peaceful space in contrast to features like the Cascade,' says the Duchess. 'The idea was to have clouds of white blossom with a carpet of 600,000 pink 'Mistress' tulips planted below.' There can be few places in the country with such an extravagance of tulips, in one colour.

'I think it is better to take people out of normal life for five minutes to think, "Wow, this is mindblowing," than make something nice but ordinary,' says the Duchess. 'We didn't want to have fifteen varieties of cherry trees with twenty varieties of tulips simply because it might last for a longer period. Our ethos, here at least, is that it is better to make someone gasp in amazement and see something that is iconic and extraordinary. We put the trees in when they were fifteen years old, but they are going to take realistically ten years to start forming a huge canopy of blossom. Then it will, I hope, be truly beautiful.'

BELOW One of the garden's volunteers, Margaret Whittaker, captured some of the 300 *Prunus* 'Taihaku' blooming in May, in imitation of the Japanese annual white cherry blossom festival. The new orchard's underplanting of a colossal 600,000 'Mistress' tulips will compete for attention as the trees mature.

THE ROSE GARDEN

David Austin Roses sponsored the huge Rose Garden by donating 3,000 plants of 180 varieties: a range of climbing, shrub, old, and English roses of every form, colour and size, chosen by Peter Wirtz, who designed the garden. The roses start flowering in late May and continue right through into the autumn until the first frosts. In season the garden is a rose lover's paradise.

There are pergolas covered in climbing roses such as 'Etoile de Hollande' and 'May Queen', as well as honeysuckle and clematis. Under one pergola, with bench seating, is a large two-hundred-year-old lead urn representing the four seasons, supported by sculptures of monkeys with one of a fox on the top.

In the rose beds, 'Anne Boleyn', 'Gertrude Jekyll', 'Queen of Denmark', 'Winchester Cathedral' and 'Graham Thomas' are among the many English favourites.

The garden also includes 'The Alnwick Rose', a new English rose created by David Austin Roses and launched at the Royal Horticultural Society's Chelsea Flower Show in 2001. This rose has a lovely cup-shaped pink flower and has, according to the company, 'a good Old Rose fragrance with just a hint of raspberry'.

BELOW Three thousand rose plants make up the Alnwick Garden's Rose Garden. The urn (right), with a fox on top, came from Syon Park.

THE SERPENT GARDEN

In the Lower Garden, next to the Rose Garden, is the Serpent Garden. Here, hiding behind a topiary serpent in holly and yew designed by Wirtz, are a variety of polished stainless-steel water sculptures by William Pye, their mirror-like surfaces reflecting the surrounding hedging.

The centrepiece is Torricelli, which works by hydrostatic pressure, its central trunk or tube filling slowly with water until its ground jets fountain into life. This is one of the many things there are in the garden for the young ones to enjoy as much as adults: in summer children like to get soaked by standing close to the tube until it fills and the jets start.

Each of the eight water sculptures is designed to show how water moves in beautiful ways. Moreover, each is particularly tactile – one cannot help touching them or poking the fingers into *The Vortex*, for example. One sculpture shows the Coanda effect. Henri Coanda, says Pye, 'has been called "the father of fluid dynamics". He was particularly intrigued by the way

LEFT AND ABOVE David Austin Roses donated the roses to the garden and created the Alnwick Rose, seen here (left) in full bloom. This cup-shaped rose has an old rose fragrance combined with a hint of raspberry.

fluids cling to surfaces. This came to be called the Coanda effect – demonstrated on an overhanging surface where the water is allowed to spill over the edge of a bowl and adhere to its underside, converging towards the central trunk.'

One of the garden's ambitions is to attract people, especially the young, who might not ordinarily be interested in horticulture or usually visit a garden. Seeing young children in this garden all excited and getting totally soaked, on a warm summer day, was evidence enough to me of success.

THE BAMBOO LABYRINTH

Perfect for a game of hide and seek, and obviously popular with children, the Bamboo Labyrinth was designed by Adrian Fisher, a British designer famous in his field of maze making. Twisting paths run through the bamboo, which rustles in the wind like scratchy tissue paper. He used five hundred *Fargesia rufa*, chosen for its profusion of lovely blue-green foliage. The bamboo will reach a height of about 8 feet/2.5 metres and just over 39 inches/1 metre in width, which suits this evergreen maze perfectly.

THE POISON GARDEN

The only entrance into the Poison Garden is through some macabre black gates with skull-and-crossbone motifs and a sign saying 'These Plants Can Kill'. The Poison Garden contains many plants we are used to seeing in gardens but makes one look and think about such plants differently. Take the ugly and common castor oil plant (*Ricinus communis*): many of us might know the story of Georgi Markov, who was shot in the leg with a poison pellet on London's Waterloo Bridge in 1978 by a secret agent using a gun hidden in an umbrella; but I did not know that the deadly poison was ricin, nor that this came from the beans of the castor oil plant. Other plants here include *Strychnos nux-vomica*, from which strychnine comes and which is grown in the Poison Garden's flame-shaped beds with the likes of belladonna, tobacco and mandrake.

The Duchess is particularly interested in poison and created this garden knowing that the ghoulish side of plants would

---

LEFT The Serpent Garden is home to water sculptures by William Pye, which the Prince of Wales, the garden's patron, visited with the Duchess (left) when he opened the second phase of the garden in September 2007, having opened the first phase in September 2002.

RIGHT The Poison Garden invites people to consider plants from an intriguing aspect, and is especially popular with children. Many banned or poisonous plants, such as strychnine, are grown here in the flame-shaped beds, and shown only on a tour, to amuse or educate.

appeal to children's imaginations. 'If you take a child into an "apothecary garden" and teach them how an aspirin's ingredient comes from the bark of a tree, many will just switch off. But if you take a child up to a strychnine plant and say: "There was a woman who was put to death in Italy for helping hundreds of women kill their husbands using this plant" they are in awe.'

The Alnwick Garden Trust also uses the plants here to work with civic organizations in helping to teach young people about the dangers of drugs. 'No one who comes here is allowed away from a guide,' says the Duchess. 'We have a Home Office licence to grow certain plants in the Poison Garden, under cloches, which produce cannabis, cocaine and magic mushrooms, and the ricin.'

THE TREEHOUSE

On the edge of the Alnwick Garden overlooking the Capability Brown landscape the Duchess built one of the largest treehouses in the world. It is made from Canadian cedar, Scandinavian redwood and English and Scots pine and sits in a copse of very tall ancient lime trees on the edge of a big dip. Because of its size it is supported by discreet wooden braces, some concrete foundations and two well-hidden solid towers.

At the heart of the Treehouse is a restaurant, which serves fresh home-made dishes and locally sourced food. The atmospheric interior is made entirely of wood, with a central log fire, trees growing through the floor, hand-made wooden furniture and twinkling fairy lights. At the top is a hideaway for private dining and small parties, and out on the deck there is a bar, serving drinks into the evening.

Behind the Treehouse are walkways with two suspension bridges – wobbly rope bridges for adults and children to bounce along, perhaps best tackled before you dine or drink.

You may be interested in the Woodland Walk path, which begins beneath the Treehouse. It is well marked and takes in views of the River Aln and of Alnwick Castle, enveloped in its quintessentially romantic Capability Brown landscape. If you are not in the mood for a long walk, just head to the nearby Duchess's Seat, as the view from here puts the geography of the castle, park and garden into the best perspective.

RIGHT Made entirely of wood, with a magical Hobbit-like atmosphere, the Treehouse is perhaps one of Britain's quirkiest restaurants.
FAR RIGHT On the edge of a dip in a copse of lime trees, the Treehouse is built from cedar, redwood and pine. Because of its size, it cannot entirely hang in the trees, so is supported by discreet wooden braces and some hidden concrete foundations and towers.

GARDEN PROJECTS

The garden provides a venue for a whole series of local community activities and projects. Anyone can go along to these, and families on holiday in Northumberland might find one of them an enjoyable distraction. Some events are educational, such as the Roots and Shoots project, where local schoolchildren grow their own vegetables, which are later made into soup for them by the chef at the Treehouse restaurant. There are also hedgehog workshops, which teach children how to make a home for these creatures to hibernate in during the winter. There are other child treats in the summer such as face-painting courses. For adults, there are courses such as 'Pot 'n' go', where you can learn how best to pot up a range of plants that are in the garden and take them home. There are 'Baby Boogie' classes that I can't quite fathom but are quite popular with young mothers, or perhaps young daddies. Other projects are aimed at older people: the Elderberries Project, for instance, which organizes tea dances in the Pavilion, or specialist guided visits for the elderly.

The Duchess is keen to stress that 'The charity is lucky enough to have a generous and wonderful volunteer taskforce who have been fundamental to the success of this project. The garden simply wouldn't have got this far without them.'

'The garden is not finished,' she explains. 'At some point, the space between the Pavilion and the Cascade needs to be fully agreed, funded and planted. Elements like the Spiral Garden, the Quiet Garden or the Garden of the Senses have been designed by Jacques Wirtz but are yet to be built. We also have plans to build for children a play area near the Treehouse. I hope it will set a new standard for play in Europe. But it is a huge, huge build with seven separate play areas all in one area, so is not going to happen overnight.' To this end all the proceeds from ticket sales are re-invested in the charity, and fund-raising activities continue.

While the 12th Duchess of Northumberland has certainly helped put Alnwick on the map, she remains pragmatic about what one person can do. 'I remember Ralph saying to me when we moved here, and when I began the garden, "Just remember one thing: don't think you will ever win – you won't. Just do your best." I have followed his advice. And despite the occasional criticism, I have come to realize that if you are worried about what people think you would never do anything in life.'

For her, plants and garden design are simply two of many motivators in creating the garden. 'I am really interested in people,' she says with emphasis, 'and ultimately, that is what this garden is about. If you are lucky enough to be able to make a small difference to life, well, you should do that. And, for oneself, you learn a lot along the way.'

HULNE PARK

If you walk upstream from the Lion Bridge, near the castle, you enter Hulne Park, one of England's greatest parks, although not well known, as it is privately managed. From the twelfth century, it was the forest of the Lord of Alnwick and by the late Middle Ages it had grown into a fine hunting ground. However, it suffered and declined in subsequent centuries until 1750, when the 1st Duke and Duchess rescued it and developed it as a huge and picturesque naturalistic pleasure ground with rides and follies, either clearing old growth or making new plantations to enhance the landscape.

The 2nd Duke extended the park and purchased Alnwick Abbey and part of its land, and planted more plantations. By 1811, his new 13-mile/21-kilometre perimeter wall around Hulne Park was complete. The 3rd Duke continued to expand the park around the Abbey, adding more walls and bridges, but the park shrunk in size. A northern highway ran through the park from Alnwick to Eglingham and when this became a turnpike in 1826, 1,500 acres/607 hectares of park were cut off. To preserve privacy a new wall was built along this road. However, the days of the park being only for the family were numbered, for the 4th Duke opened Hulne Park to the inhabitants of Alnwick in 1847. In addition, old plantations throughout the park were enlarged with oak, larch, Scots fir and spruce. A 1854 Act of Parliament gave the 4th Duke a section of Alnwick Moor (237 acres/96 hectares), which was absorbed into the park on the western side.

Successive Percy generations have enjoyed the buildings, monuments, woodlands, drive and shooting of game birds in the park, while making the odd change here and there. The 10th Duke was especially diligent in maintaining the park – a tradition that his son wholeheartedly continues, and much enjoys. Indeed the two most outstanding buildings in the park, Brizlee Tower and Hulne Priory, are now restored and both used constantly in the shooting season.

Shooting missed out on the estate after the First World War, as both the Duke's grandparents and parents were keener on foxhunting. A passionate sportsman, widely regarded as an outstanding shot, the present Duke has a profound understanding of wildlife and cares for it. The Duke also loves his fishing but, like his wife and children, is not so keen to ride to hounds.

Led by the Duke, an important part of Northumberland Estates' work is game and wildlife management, as part of a nature conservation programme to enhance the castle's home shoot, Hulne Park, but also to support wildlife on other parts

started with only seventeen pairs. A thousand birds are considered enough to provide a harvestable surplus for a shoot. To achieve and maintain these numbers various changes were made, including the introduction of conservation headlands around all the fields that must not be sprayed with herbicides or insecticides. Set-aside policies on the fields were changed to be more bird friendly. Bird habitat was improved, extra hedging was planted and hedge bases better protected. Winter field stubble was left as long as possible and night-time work on fields was reduced to avoid disturbing the birds. The cutting of grass at the fields' edges was also kept to the minimum. This encouraged insects to flourish, which in turn helped provide food for young birds. The benefits to wildlife in general have been good. The numbers of hares as well as wild pheasant, hedge sparrow, lapwing, skylark, chaffinch and yellow hammer have dramatically increased since the start of the project.

For those who like long walks the Duke introduced four areas around Alnwick town, including three circular routes within Hulne Park, by joining existing footpaths with new sections of pathways to make the land more accessible. The estate worked hard to clear paths, put in new gates and stiles and add waymarker badges to prevent walkers from getting lost. 'We are lucky to be surrounded by some beautiful countryside and parkland,' said the Duke, 'so I hope these routes will make it easier for people to get out and enjoy it.'

HULNE PRIORY

Perched on a grassy hill in Alnwick's beautiful park, surrounded by forest, is Hulne Priory. Within the remains of this isolated priory is a ravishingly rare Robert Adam hunting lodge, a fine example of Gothic Revival style in the Rococo period.

When the Carmelites fled to Europe and England in the thirteenth century, many bishops were reluctant to have these barefoot friars, who were dedicated to prayer, poverty and celibacy, in their dioceses. But fortunately William de Vesci, Baron of Alnwick, granted the order a home in what was then the forest of Alnwick in 1242, apparently because one of the novices, a crusader-turned-hermit called Ralph Fresborn, had grown up in Northumberland. The friars built Hulne Priory, using local stone from the Alnwick moors.

In 1488 the 4th Earl, Henry Percy, added the Great Tower in memory of his wife, Maud. Three floors high and with battlements, it cost £27 19s. Above the main fireplace is an inscription to her that reads: 'This towr was bilded by Sir Hen Percy, that espoused Maud ye good lady full of virtue.' Adjacent to the priory, the Great Tower served as the 4th

of the estate. With the help of gamekeepers, the estate works to improve biodiversity. For example, it is determined to help red squirrels maintain their presence in the park in the face the invasion of grey squirrels. Beehives are also encouraged. The keepered area of the estate overall is 22,000 acres/8,903 hectares. Active management of the land for shooting and fishing helps conserve Hulne Park's landscape and the balance of wildlife, and includes a programme of predator control to support biodiversity. This involves efforts to prevent vermin from eating all the birds' eggs and keeping the rabbit population within reasonable levels.

The Duke's wild grey partridge project took three seasons to encourage bird numbers to reach over a thousand, having

ABOVE The Duke's mother commented that when she married, 'One had to throw oneself into what the Percys liked doing. Every Percy fished all their lives.' The Duke is no exception. A keen fisherman, here he is proudly showing a salmon.

Earl's shooting lodge, as Hulne Park was – and still is – a prime hunting ground. With the War of the Roses a recent memory and Scots raiding the borders of England, the tower also became a place of refuge and the high wall that was built around the priory stands intact.

During the upheaval of the Reformation the priory church was demolished on the orders of Henry VIII. Fortunately, some buildings were left intact, including the Great Tower, but the ruined priory fell under the control of the Crown. By the mid-eighteenth century, however, it was back in Percy hands, and the ruins became the favourite sporting haunt of the 1st Duke and Duchess, Hugh and Elizabeth.

After the 1st Duchess died in 1776, her husband, remembering her love of carriage rides, with the priory her favourite destination, employed Robert Adam to renovate the priory's Great Tower in her memory. Since she had employed Adam to work at both Alnwick Castle and Syon House it was natural for the Duke to ask him to help at the priory. Sandstone was used for the carved interior masonry, but for the outside walls stone from the Alnwick moors was used.

Adam also built a two-storey picnic house overlooking the ruined cloisters and the Duchess's recently planted garden. He designed this with a corridor connecting it to the old tower. On the ground floor was a reception room – now empty – that was used for picnics under cover. Upstairs was a drawing room. To create a high dining room in the tower, Adam knocked out the upper floor. He then designed the dining room and the picnic room in the same style, with plasterwork. Outside, two round medallion Coadestone portraits of the Duke and Duchess flanked the first-floor drawing-room window.

Today little has changed from Robert Adam's time. After problems of leaking lead roofs and wet and dry rot, today the hunting lodge is fully restored. The huge Gothic windows, with their curved timber, had rotted, and it took George Tate, the joiner, months to remake them, using only hand tools. Ornate plasterwork was copied with moulds and the rotten wooden strips and hessian underneath the plaster replaced. Now the Duke and Duchess use the lodge frequently for shooting lunches.

LEFT The romantic and isolated Hulne Priory was restored by the Duchess after 1995 and is today used for shooting lunches. The interiors are a fine example of the revived Gothic style by Robert Adam, where animal heads from the 9th Duke's 1930s safaris are displayed. This dining room is in the Great Tower added to the original Carmelite priory by the 4th Earl in 1488.
ABOVE With Henry VIII's Dissolution of the Monasteries in the late 1530s, much of the priory was destroyed but the stone entrance remains.

Inside the newer eighteenth-century Picnic House, the wooden staircase leading upstairs is next to an ancient grave slab, probably of a crusading knight, embellished with a simple carved sword beside a thirteenth-century Celtic-style cross. Next to the tombstone is the entrance to the bare downstairs picnic room with a simple oak-planked floor, a fine fireplace, plain walls but beautiful plasterwork in the Strawberry Hill or, as some people call it, 'Fairy Gothick' style – a fine and fanciful, almost Rococo style.

Upstairs, on the left is the drawing room, with two armchairs and a fine Adam fireplace, made of local Denwick sandstone, with the carved crescents used in the Percy coat of arms. Leading off the drawing room is a simple kitchen and a wine cellar. Along the first-floor corridor, past a stone staircase that leads to the turret roof, you enter the Great Tower. Inside this is Adam's double-height dining room with two grand Gothic windows, their surrounds and cornicing embellished with fine, white-painted plasterwork.

The walls are painted in a simple but warm gold-yellow and the doors are painted in oil eggshell in black. The yellow walls are 'limewash tinted yellow', limewash being the type

ABOVE After his wife died, the 1st Duke demolished a floor in the 4th Earl's Great Tower to create the double-height dining room, with two grand Gothic windows, this one looking out on to the park and its grazing sheep.

RIGHT The walls are painted 'limewash tinted yellow' for a chalky warm effect and to best show the ravishing plasterwork, all restored by the Duchess. The chairs are covered in a tartan-like Percy tweed, which was originally woven for use by the estate gamekeepers.

RIGHT AND OPPOSITE When the Percy heiress and 1st Duchess died in 1776, her husband, Hugh, built the 85-foot/26-metre-high Brizlee Tower in the middle of Hulne Park in her memory. The Grade I-listed building is said to have been designed by Robert Adam in 1777 and completed in 1781. Some attribute more of the design to James Adam or to the 1st Duke. Either way, the arches, niches and fluted columns are perfect examples of the eighteenth-century Gothic Revival style. The current Duke (right) extensively restored the tower after 2000.

of 'moisture-breathable' paint used in the eighteenth century and now used in conservation in older buildings. The yellow colour was hand mixed on site, predominantly with ochre, and endorsed by the current Duchess, who likes the warm effect.

In the dining room is a splendid long table with Percy tartan-covered chairs. 'The fabric isn't strictly a tartan,' says the Duchess, 'but a Percy tweed which we had woven for use by the estate gamekeepers (an old tradition on sporting estates). The black and white tartan is the Northumberland county tartan and is still used by the Duke's piper.'

The big change inside is the addition on the walls of animal heads, mostly shot overseas in the 1920s and '30s by the Duke's uncle. There are also skins of lion, water buffalo, cheetah, leopard and more, all hung with a fine eye. Labels tell you where each was shot – from Ladakh in India to Dalnessie Forest in the Scottish Highlands. They had been languishing in storage until the Duchess suggested they be moved to the hunting lodge. Their superb condition is attributed to the hand of the taxidermist Roland Ward, and usefully, says the Duchess, 'they improve the acoustics'.

'We absolutely love it here,' she says. 'This is a very special place and it has the most wonderful atmosphere. Mind you, it has no central heating, but we have the fires lit in the morning so it gets quite cosy by lunchtime.'

As you leave the grounds of the priory, along the inside of the north surrounding walls there is a collection of small upright gravestones. They are relatively recent and inscribed with the names and dates of the Duke and Duchess's dogs. The most recent addition is that of Missy's much-loved Frank, the Duke and Duchess's younger daughter's Norfolk terrier, who died in 2011.

While the interior of Hulne Priory is private, Hulne Park and the castle grounds are open to the public, on foot only, except during shoots.

BRIZLEE TOWER

'Greatest of all the [1st] duke's monuments built in the memory of his duchess was Brizlee Tower,' says Colin Shrimpton, the castle's retired archivist, in his book *A History of Alnwick Parks and Pleasure Grounds*.

This circular tower is in the middle of Hulne Park, off Tower Drive on top of Brizlee Hill. From the top, the views are spectacular: west to the Cheviots, 20 miles/32 kilometres away; northwards, over Hulne Park's valley 436 feet/133 metres below and the winding River Aln; east to the Northumberland coast. South of the tower the views are blocked by the Alnwick moors, which are even higher.

The folly has at least six storeys and is 85 feet/26 metres high. At the top is a cast-iron octagonal fire basket from which a beacon can be lit. By tradition, this is done when a Duchess of Northumberland gives birth to a male heir.

Like the Picnic House at the Priory, the tower is said to be designed by Robert Adam in 1777 and completed in 1781. However, some attribute the design to John Adam or to the 1st Duke. Either way, the cusped and crocketed arches, arched niches and fluted columns are perfect examples of the Gothic Revival style. Slim and elegant, with ashlar masonry, the tower is decorated with fretted mouldings. 'As a final touch, the tower was embellished with roundel portraits, moulded in white Coade stone, of the duke and duchess,' explains Colin Shrimpton.

By the end of the twentieth century the Grade I listed tower had suffered extensive water damage and corroding ironwork. The Duke and Duchess spent a great sum restoring it.

On the walls of the tower's first balcony is a plaque, which Colin Shrimpton says is 'carved with a Latin inscription chosen by the 1st Duke to record his considerable achievements'. It means: 'Look about you; I have measured all these things; they are my orders; it is my planning; many of the trees have been planted by my own hand.'

THE GRAVEYARD

Since the eighteenth century the Dukes and Duchesses of Northumberland have been buried in Westminster Abbey, but now there is only one space left, reserved for Duchess Elizabeth, widow of the 10th Duke.

Known for their forward planning, the Duke and Duchess therefore needed to find a new burial ground for the Percys and created one up along the hill from Brizlee Tower. The view from the graveyard west, over the valley below, is breathtaking. The 10th Duke and Duchess took the Queen and Prince Philip up here in May 1982, to show them this highlight of Hulne Park.

The burial ground is square, protected by four walls made of stone from Alnwick Moor. The Duke and Duchess

commissioned the artist and blacksmith Stephen Lunn to make the gates. 'He is a genius,' the Duchess says. He uses traditional methods of hot forging to express his inspirations drawn from nature in the form of modern contemporary designs. The 12-foot/3.5-metre gates won him the Worshipful Company of Blacksmiths' Tonypandy Cup (named after Lord Tonypandy, a former Speaker of the House of Commons), awarded for outstanding workmanship.

The double gates are made from mild steel dipped in molten zinc, cleaned and then spray painted with seven coats of paint. One side of the gate is dedicated to the Duke and the other to the Duchess. The Duke's side has grouse or fish emblems, reflecting his interesting in shooting, wildlife and fishing. The Duchess's side has garden and floral motifs plus a skull that she wanted incorporated into the design. There is also an owl on top of one of the gates, which, as Stephen explains, 'draws the eye upwards'.

In the centre of the graveyard is an intricate sculpture of a birch tree, made from stainless steel by Stephen. Copper strips wrapped round it imitate the birch's peeling bark. Five birds forged out of solid stainless steel sit on the tree branches. The metal roots are firmly wrapped on a massive slab of stone on which the tree sculpture rests.

'I think the new graveyard is probably one of the most important things that we have done here,' says the 12th Duchess. 'This is the final resting place of the Dukes of the future, their wives and their immediate family. And on this wonderful secluded hilltop in Hulne Park looking west towards the Cheviots it is the best location we could think of.' While the ground has been consecrated, the new graveyard is so far empty of bones. I only hope that it is not put to use for some time.

LEFT These fine gates made by the artist and blacksmith Stephen Lunn protect the new family graveyard in the middle of Hulne Park, on a hill looking west towards the Cheviots.

ABOVE LEFT The Duke's mother, a keen photographer, took this photograph in May 1982 when she and her husband, the 10th Duke, took the Queen and Prince Philip up here to show them the views over Hulne Park.

ABOVE RIGHT The Duke and Duchess had the new graveyard consecrated early in 2010.

PAGE 236 From the new graveyard the view north-west passes over the park to Alnwick Moor and beyond, clouds hiding the Cheviot Hills.

Select Bibliography

Allibone, Jill, *Anthony Salvin: Pioneer of Gothic Revival Architecture*, Lutterworth Press, 1988

August, Ian, *The Making of the Alnwick Garden*, Pavilion, 2006

Bagot, Sophia Louisa Percy, *Links with the Past*, 1901

Baird, Rosemary, *Mistress of the House: Great Ladies and Grand Houses 1670–1830*, Weidenfeld & Nicolson, 2003

Davison, W., *A Descriptive and Historical View of Alnwick and of Alnwick Castle*, Davison, 1822

De Courcy, Anne, *Debs at War: How Wartime Changed their Lives 1939 1945*, Weidenfeld & Nicolson, 2005

De Fonblanque, E.B., *Annals of the House of Percy*, 1887

Dolan, Brian, *Ladies of the Grand Tour*, Harper Collins, 2001

Donaldson, T.L., *Brief Memoir of the Late Commendatore Canina*, RIBA Transactions, 1856–7

Ewing, Heather, *The Lost World of James Smithson*, Bloomsbury, 2007

French, Anne, *Art Treasures in the North: Northern Families on the Grand Tour*, Unicorn, 2009

Greig, James (ed.), *The Diaries of a Duchess*, Hodder and Stoughton, 1926

Grose, F., *The Antiquities of England and Wales*, 1775

Harris, Eileen, *The Genius of Robert Adam: His Interiors*, Yale University Press, 2001

Hartshorne, C.H., *A Guide to Alnwick Castle*, Longmans, Green, Reader, & Dyer, 1865

Hugonin, Bill, *Alnwick 1960–1990: A Personal Memoir*, Alnwick Castle Private Archives, 2010

Jenkins, Simon, *England's Thousand Best Houses*, Penguin, 2003

Lees-Milne, James, *The Age of Adam*, B.T. Batsford Ltd, 1947

Matthew, Colin (ed.), *Oxford Dictionary of National Biography*, Oxford University Press, 1992

Montgomery-Massingberd, Hugh, *Great Houses of England and Wales*, Laurence King, 1994

Musson, Jeremy, *Up and Down Stairs: The History of the Country House Servant*, John Murray, 2010

Northumberland, Alan Ian, 8th Duke of, *Guide-Book to Alnwick Castle*, W.M. Blackwood & Sons Ltd, 1930

Northumberland, Ralph, 12th Duke of, 'Looking Ahead', *Percy News*, April 1996

Percy, Algernon, *A Bearskin's Crimea*, Leo Cooper, 2005

Plumptre, James (ed. Ian Ousby), *James Plumptre's Britain: The Journals of a Tourist in the 1790s*, Hutchinson, 1992

Rowell, Christopher, *Petworth House*, National Trust, 1997

Shrimpton, Colin, *A History of Alnwick Parks and Pleasure Grounds*, Heritage House Group, 2006

—, *Alnwick Castle*, Heritage House Group, 2008

—, 'The Spirit of the Place', *Percy News*, October 1999

Sykes, Christopher Simon, *Private Palaces: Life in the Great London Houses*, Chatto and Windus, 1985

Williams Wynn, Frances, *Diaries of a Lady of Quality from 1797 to 1844*, Longman, Green, Longman, Roberts & Green, 1864

Index
Page numbers in *italic* refer to captions

ACKNOWLEDGMENTS

First, I owe a debt of gratitude to the Duke and Duchess of Northumberland for their inspiration and for their hospitality to *l'artiste en résidence*. A special acknowledgment is due to the Dowager Duchess Elizabeth, for her illuminating conversations, and for permission to source material from her scrapbooks and photographs.

I am especially grateful to Clare Baxter, Lisa Little and Christopher Hunwick in the Collections and Archives Department for their interviews, knowledge and advice on the text. I acknowledge with great thanks the written works of their retired colleague Colin Shrimpton and also the guide Daniel Watkins for his 'Guide to the Percy Family and its History'. I would also like to thank the following for their valued input: Lucy Manners, Bill Hugonin, Algernon Percy, Ian August, Robin Smeaton, Gillian Millar, Andrew Farquharson, Brinley Moralee, Dr Adiano Aymonimo, Michael Johnson and Tom Patterson.

For help with various tasks, I thank Terry and Colin Geary, Helen McDonald, Cosmo Trevelyan Brockway, Laurence Tucker, Anna Peters and Liz Cornwell. When researching in Rome, I appreciated the help and company of Hamish Bowles.

I am grateful to Kate Devlin for her help with the estate's art image library, to Margaret Whittaker for allowing me to use some of her garden images, to Mark Mather for his photographs of Katie's wedding, and to Ian Jones and Jane Coltman for their images of recent royal visits.

A special thank you to my family – Ian, Janet, Helen, Patrick and Suzie McDonald – and all my friends, for their patience and encouragement.

Finally, much appreciation is due to Becky Clarke, who designed the book, and to Andrew Dunn, editorial director of Frances Lincoln, for being so bold as to take me on. Above all, it is impossible to overstate what I owe to my editor, Anne Askwith.

PICTURE CREDITS

I am extremely grateful to the following for permission to include their work in my book, to supplement my own; to *World of Interiors* for permission to reuse the photograph I took for them; and to Northumberland Estates for copyright permission to reproduce images of numerous paintings.

Pages 9, 41 right, 42, 198: copyright © Mark Mather 2011
Page 33: Cecil Beaton/*Vogue* copyright © Condé Nast Publications 1937
Pages 43, 211, 218 right, 219: copyright © Margaret Whittaker 2011
Page 200: James McDonald copyright © *World of Interiors* 2009
Page 209: copyright © Ian Jones 2012
Page 222 lower right: copyright © Jane Coltman 2007